Anatomy of a Civil War

Anatomy of a Civil War demonstrates the destructive nature of war, ranging from the physical destruction to a range of psychosocial problems to the detrimental effects on the environment. Despite such horrific aspects of war, evidence suggests that civil war is likely to generate multilayered outcomes. To examine the transformative aspects of civil war, Mehmet Gurses draws on an original survey conducted in Turkey, where a Kurdish armed group, the Kurdistan Workers' Party (PKK), has been waging an intermittent insurgency for Kurdish self-rule since 1984. Findings from a probability sample of 2,100 individuals randomly selected from three major Kurdish-populated provinces in the eastern part of Turkey, coupled with insights from face-to-face in-depth interviews with dozens of individuals affected by violence, provide evidence for the multifaceted nature of exposure to violence during civil war. Just as the destructive nature of war manifests itself in various forms and shapes, wartime experiences can engender positive attitudes toward women, create a culture of political activism, and develop secular values at the individual level. Nonetheless, changes in gender relations and the rise of a secular political culture appear to be primarily shaped by wartime experiences interacting with insurgent ideology.

Mehmet Gurses is Associate Professor of Political Science at Florida Atlantic University.

ANATOMY OF A CIVIL WAR

*Sociopolitical Impacts of the
Kurdish Conflict in Turkey*

Mehmet Gurses

University of Michigan Press
Ann Arbor

Published in the United States of America by the
University of Michigan Press
Manufactured in the United States of America
Printed on acid-free paper

A CIP catalog record for this book is available from the British Library.

Library of Congress Cataloging-in-Publication Data

Names: Gurses, Mehmet, author.
Title: Anatomy of a civil war : sociopolitical impacts of the Kurdish conflict in Turkey /
    Mehmet Gurses.
Description: Ann Arbor : University of Michigan Press, 2018. | Includes bibliographical
    references and index.
Identifiers: LCCN 2018021268 (print) | LCCN 2018029536 (ebook) | ISBN
    9780472124282 (E-book) | ISBN 9780472131006 (hardback)
Subjects: LCSH: Kurds—Turkey—Politics and government. | Kurds—Turkey—History—
    Autonomy and independence movements. | Partiya Karkerãen Kurdistanãe—History. |
    Turkey—Politics and government—1980– | Turkey—Ethnic relations. | Insurgency—
    Case studies. | Civil wars—Case studies. | BISAC: POLITICAL SCIENCE /
    International Relations / General. | POLITICAL SCIENCE / Peace. | SOCIAL
    SCIENCE / Women's Studies. Classification: LCC DR435.K87 (ebook) | LCC DR435.
    K87 G886 2018 (print) | DDC 956.1/00491597—dc23
LC record available at https://lccn.loc.gov/2018021268

To
T. David Mason, a great mentor and a true scholar,
and Sosin for her enduring love . . .

Contents

Preface

Over the course of the past four decades, much has changed in Turkey and the Middle East. Despite a dubious beginning, the Kurdistan Workers' Party (PKK), which in the 1970s could best be described as just another Kurdish group formed by a few adventurous college students, has managed to grow into one of the most powerful substate actors in Turkey and beyond. It has come to present the most serious challenge to the Turkish state since its foundation in 1923. Moreover, through the PKK's offshoots or groups it has inspired in neighboring Syria and Iraq, it has become the United States' most effective on-the-ground ally in the fight against radical Islamism.

Significantly, it has become a "social movement industry," engendering several nonviolent organizations at both the local and national levels. It has given rise to the Peoples' Democratic Party (HDP), which received support from millions of Kurds as well as a minority of Turkish liberals and leftists in the June 7, 2015 elections, and won 80 seats in the 550-seat national assembly. Its fraternal party, the Peace and Democracy Party (BDP), swept the polls in the Kurdish-dominated East in the 2014 municipal elections. The insurgency has also stimulated a number of women's groups with radical feminist agendas and has laid the groundwork for local committees to be formed and effectively participate in their localities. This book is an attempt to explore the social and political outcomes of the PKK insurgency that has fundamentally changed the Kurdish society. In a larger sense, however, *Anatomy of a Civil War* is about the transformative aspects of armed conflict, and I thus hope to tie the Kurdish case to the larger literature on war and change.

While the journey of this book has been long and arduous, it has also been life-changing for me. This has been a work in the making for quite some time as I was struggling to make sense of my own personal transformation. Over the past few years, as I revisited Kurdish cities and towns in eastern Turkey, conversed with hundreds of people who suffered because of the armed conflict, listened to personal, intimate, touching, and painful stories of many who had lost their daughters, sons, sisters, brothers, or friends, I came to realize that the conflict dynamics have created an insistent personality, demanding, not begging, for justice, in spite of the physical and psychosocial costs the three-decade insurgency has produced. Importantly, Kurdish women who not so long ago were largely "absent" from the public life had risen to be mayors, parliamentarians, party leaders, and fighters. They were asserting themselves not just as Kurds but also as women. Religion was being redefined; fewer people were referring to Islam in identifying themselves. People from all walks of life, educated and illiterates and urbanities and peasants alike, were constantly making references to such modern concepts as "democracy," "liberty," and "gender equality." Despite, at times, the lack of a deep understanding of what such concepts actually entailed, this picture was emerging from a region where unspeakable atrocities were being committed on a daily basis at the hands of sworn enemies of the above-mentioned notions, radical Islamists.

First and foremost, I am appreciative of the dozens of Kurdish women and men who agreed to share their painful experiences with me. Listening to their stories was both difficult and transformational. As the words fail to properly convey my gratitude, I respectfully take a bow before your pain and resolve.

This research project would not have been possible without the invaluable help and contributions of many I proudly deem as my mentors, colleagues, and friends. While I received no major external grants for this research, I was fortunate to obtain some internal support from my institution, Florida Atlantic University. Specifically, the sabbatical leave I was granted in Fall semester 2015 provided me with the time necessary to refine my arguments and travel to Canada, Belgium, and Turkey to gather face-to-face interview data.

I owe a special debt of gratitude to two individuals, Zeki Mert and Erdogan Atas, who through their financial contributions facilitated this project. In fact, they, as two individuals who have been victimized by the very same conflict, typify the positive outcomes depicted in this book. Zeki Mert, who arrived in Canada as a refugee in the late 1990s, serves as an example of suffering-turned-strength. Zeki, a family man, father of three children, has built a successful business in Toronto. Whereas Erdogan, despite a humble beginning and against all odds, has launched a lucrative business in the United States. Without their generous assistance, this journey would have been longer and more laborious.

I am also thankful to Roni Research, a public-opinion research company based in Istanbul, in particular to its manager, Mr. Harun Okur, for their time and resources in collecting the survey data that constitutes the main part of the empirical analysis presented in this book. My thanks also go to Mehmet Akdag for introducing me to Roni Research.

I also owe a debt of gratitude to Aimee Arias, Jackie Nichols, Mirya Holman, Angela Nichols, Jeffrey Morton, Dukhong Kim, Kevin Wagner, Tim Lenz, Gail Choate, Chris William Johnson, Nicolas Rost, Nicolai Petrovsky, Ahmed Arif, Sertac Tekin, Heval Pektas, Recep Aslan, Himan Hosseini, Yousif Ismael, Kamal Soleimani, Ekrem Karakoc, Zeki Sarigil, Sabri Ciftci, and Murat Tezcur for offering their insights, time, and support during this voyage. Moreover, I would like to thank Eli, Sercan, Rengin, Miro, Eziz, Newzad, Ekrem, Ercan, H. Merxendi, Cengiz, Cevdet, Zeynep, Naif, and Nevzat for their invaluable assistance, friendship, and generosity during my visits to Canada, Belgium, and Turkey. My thanks also go to my editors at the University of Michigan Press for their keen interest in the proposal from the early stages and for their responsible and responsive attitudes throughout the review and publication processes.

As I was working on the statistical parts of the book, I realized how lucky I had been for having a mentor like Patrick T. Brandt, who worked tirelessly to help us move through the zigzags of empirical analysis. John Booth, Michael Greig, and Andrew Enterline all have contributed to this project through their mentorship. Finally, as words cannot express my gratitude to T. David Mason, a great mentor and a true scholar, I dedicate this book to him.

Introduction

The Kurds, with an estimated population of thirty-five to forty million, are the fourth-largest ethnic group in the Middle East, but their division between Turkey, Iran, Iraq, and Syria has turned them into ethnic minorities in all four countries. Today, they make up roughly 20 percent of the total populations in both Turkey and Iraq and 10 percent of the total populations in Iran and Syria.[1] Their large, concentrated numbers dispersed across four political boundaries, coupled with repressive and assimilationist policies of the various governments, have resulted in numerous uprisings and rebellions.

Central governments have often labeled Kurdish revolts as feudal disturbances, banditry, or an obstacle on the road to forging mononationalist identities. Kurdish demands for equality have been dismissed as a foreign plot, a threat to the unity and order when they weren't ruthlessly suppressed. In the 1960s, the Syrian security police chief in the Kurdish province of Haseke (Jazira) described the Kurdish question as "a malignant tumor" that required removal (Gunter 2016, 101). The Turkish official discourse maintains that some unspecified "foreign power(s)" is behind the so-called Kurdish question (Guida 2008). Further, in 1987, the Turkish interior minister stated that the only people prepared to call themselves Kurds are "militants, tool of foreign ideologies" (McDowall 2004, 433). Nearly three decades later, in 2014, an official of the Islamic Republic of Iran warned the Kurds of the danger of an independent Kurdish state and accused them of playing into the "enemy's" hands.[2]

The Kurds received especially harsh treatment at the hands of the elites of the new Turkish Republic. Upon the formation of modern Turkey in 1923, a country home to more than half of the total Kurdish population, Turkey's founding father Kemal Ataturk and his followers, intent on forging national unity around Turkish identity, pursued assimilationist policies and rabidly anti-Kurdish state practices. In order to suppress Kurdish identity and culture, these policies denied that the Kurds were a separate nationality, criminalized the Kurdish language, and diluted the Kurdish-populated provinces through migration. These oppressive and discriminatory strategies continued without respite throughout the twentieth century (Olson 1989a; McDowall 2004; Gunter 2004; Romano 2006).

A series of failed attempts for better status, betrayals, and broken promises has given rise to a widely quoted expression that "Kurds have no friends but the mountains," which have historically served as a refuge against foreign invasion and persecution.[3] A partial list of Kurdish uprisings, all of which were brutally repressed, includes the Kocgiri revolt of the 1920s; the Sheik Said rebellion of 1925; the revolt of Agri Dagh in the 1930s; the Dersim uprising of 1937–38 in Turkey; the Simko rebellion of the 1920s; the 1946 Mahabad Republic of Kurdistan in Iran; the Barzani-led revolts of the 1960s and 1970s in Iraq; and the short, albeit significant, 2004 uprising, Serhildan, in Syria. This bloody and repressive history illustrates the long history of violence surrounding the Kurds (Olson 1989a; 1989b; McDowall 2004; Jwaideh 2006; Lowe 2010).

Today, after surviving a "lost" century of denial and subjugation, Kurds are enjoying a political resurgence in part because of the dramatic changes taking place in the countries in which they reside. Most notably, the collapse of central governments in Iraq and Syria together with Kurdish organizational readiness and fighting prowess has ushered in a growing sense of optimism that the Kurds' time might have arrived.[4] The turn of the twenty-first century, as one scholar put it, has "marked a quantum leap" for the Kurds" (Bengio 2017, 84).

The Kurds in Iraq, who gained official recognition in the 2005 constitution, have not only solidified their gains of the 1990s but have also emerged as a key player in the new Iraq and an invaluable partner of the United States (U.S.) in stabilizing and democratizing the country (Romano and Gurses 2014). The onset of the Syrian civil war in 2011, with the ensuing violence and state collapse, brought a hitherto largely unknown group, the Kurdish Democratic Union Party (Partiya Yekitiya Demokrat, PYD), to the forefront of regional and global politics.

The heroic resistance of Kurdish fighters from the People's Defense Units (Yekîneyên Parastina Gel, YPG) and the Women's Defense Units

(Yekîneyên Parastina Jin, YPJ), armed forces aligned with the PYD, during the months-long siege of Kobani in late 2014 against the onslaught of the Islamic State (IS)[5] proved to be a turning point for the Kurds in Syria. After months of intense street fighting in this Kurdish town in northern Syria, the Kurdish forces backed by U.S. airpower pushed the IS out and destroyed its aura of invincibility. The Battle of Kobani marked the beginning of a strategic partnership between the United States and the Kurds, an alliance that has become increasingly stronger over the years. It has turned the Kurdish PYD into the United States' most effective and reliable on-the-ground partner in the fight against the IS and a potentially useful force in bringing an end to the ongoing civil war.

The Kurdish forces' competence and tenacity have earned them nearly celebrity recognition in the Western media (Toivanen and Baser 2016). In addition to their military gains on the battlefield, their progressive democratic ideals and practices place them in stark contrast to the IS, a group responsible for horrendous acts including relegating women to second-class citizenship and treating them as sex slaves. The PYD's women units, which make up close to 40 percent of Kurdish fighters and have been compared to the armed Mujeres Libres (Free Women) during the Spanish Civil War in the late 1930s (Graeber 2014), were instrumental in pushing the IS out of Kobani in January 2015.

The PYD's emphasis on gender equality along with their calls for a secular, decentralized system in which different ethnic and religious groups might live together in harmony have made the Kurdish-administered cantons in northern Syria a beacon of hope in a region characterized by turmoil and bloodshed (Argentieri 2015; Holmes 2015; Knapp, Flach, and Ayboga 2016; Tax 2016a). One observer describes the emerging Kurdish entity in Syria as "the Syrian force with the most democratic, pluralistic, and feminist vision" (Tax 2016b).

The purpose of this book is to document, assess, and analyze the Kurdish struggle for equality and, more importantly, the role this struggle has played in transforming the Kurdish society, with an emphasis placed on the armed conflict between the Kurdistan Workers' Party (Partiya Karkeren Kurdistan, PKK) and Turkey.

The emphasis on the PKK insurgency, as one of the longest and most complicated ethnic armed conflicts[6] in the post World War II era, is justified on two main grounds. One relates to the PKK's impressive resilience and ability to survive and adapt to a constantly shifting environment over the course of four decades. The PKK, which was started by a small group of college students in the 1970s, has survived the Turkish government's repression as well as the capture of its leader, Abdullah Ocalan, in 1999. It has grown into one of the most powerful nonstate actors in Turkey and the region. Through its affiliates in neighboring Syria, Iraq, and Iran, as well as a number of Western countries, the PKK has come to present the most serious challenge to the Turkish state since its foundation in 1923 (Barkey and Fuller 1998; Olson 2001; Somer 2005; Gurses 2015a; White 2015). It has also inspired and influenced groups[7] that have become the United States' most effective on-the-ground partners in the fight against the Islamic State in Syria and Iraq.

The other justification is the equally remarkable social and political changes that the PKK has engendered over the years despite an unfavorable environment and culture. This aspect of the PKK deserves elaboration, as it separates the PKK insurgency from other cases that have been the subject of numerous studies seeking to delineate the link between conflict and change.

The PKK resembles such insurgent groups as the Communist Party of Nepal (Maoist) (CPN(M)), the Farabundo Marti National Liberation Front (Frente Farabundo Martí para la Liberación Nacional, FMLN) in El Salvador, or the National Resistance Army (NRA) in Uganda, which were characterized by restraint, discipline, and control. The PKK lacks, however, what some rebel movements enjoyed during their often protracted wars: liberated zones. While territorial control ranges along a continuum (Kalyvas 2006), it entails engaging in a variety of governance activities such as providing security, regulating market transactions, meeting the education and health needs of the civilian population, resolving civil disputes, and addressing other social problems that commonly accompany conflict situations (Mampilly 2011, 4).

The administration of liberated territories can have significant outcomes. It provides a base to train, plan, and regroup; it greatly shapes the characteristics of postinsurgent political parties (Lyons 2016); and it allows insurgent groups to develop strong relations with civilian populations and enforce radical social reforms. For example, in Nepal the People's Liberation Army (PLA), the armed wing of the CPN(M), enacted radical social reforms aimed at forging cross-caste alliances and ending caste discrimination practices in several "liberated" villages during the civil war of 1996–2006. "Home entry" programs, which encouraged members of the lowest caste to enter the homes of higher-caste villagers; intercaste marriages; and "forcing" members of different castes to use a single tap, have produced mixed results (Bownas 2015). The control of these territories nonetheless provided the insurgent group with an important opportunity to introduce social change.

The PKK, as a powerful insurgency, poses a serious challenge to the Turkish state's control in the Kurdish countryside (Aydin and Emrence 2015). But unlike the Liberation Tigers Tamil Eelam (LTTE) in Sri Lanka or the NRA in Uganda, the PKK lacks insurgent-controlled territory in Turkey, which has prevented it from developing a comprehensive governance system. In contrast to some civil wars fought against weak or deficient governments, the PKK has engaged in an armed conflict against a strong state with an army collectively ranked as the second largest military force in NATO. Turkey has also largely enjoyed European and American diplomatic, military, and intelligence support in its fight against the PKK insurgency.

Furthermore, this case does not have the prior domestic women's mobilization that was a factor attributed to postconflict women's rights in Uganda (Tripp 2000). It does have an Islamic culture and low levels of socioeconomic development that are negatively tied to developing a democratic culture and secularization (Inkeles and Smith 1974; Norris and Inglehart 2004; Gelner 1992; Huntington 1996). When the PKK armed struggle began in the early 1980s, the Kurdish region of Turkey was largely isolated from the rest of the country (and the world), resulting in a relative backwardness that has not changed over the years.[8] The Kurdish provinces are still predominantly agrarian and among the poorest in the country, resembling what Horowitz terms a backward group in a backward region (2000, 233–34).

The changes described here have taken place in a Muslim majority society often characterized by patriarchy, political submission, and obedience. The traditional Muslim attitude toward politics, as Brown (2000, 60–61) aptly observes, is "pessimistic" and "submissive." The long history of Islamic political thought, Brown points out, has largely resulted in preferring "suffering in silence" to "bringing the matter to the attention of political authority," which has in effect "fostered a de facto separation of state and society." Thus, inaction or the lack of belief in bringing about change, rather than "an affirmation that things can be corrected by group political activity," better describes the Muslim approach to change. Moreover, Turkey is located in a geographical area described as "the patriarchal belt" (Caldwell 1982) or the belt of "classic patriarchy" (Kandiyoti 1988), characterized by strict sexual division of labor, male domination, early marriage, and sex segregation.[9]

Clearly these attributes make this case an unlikely candidate for experiencing the sociopolitical changes described in this book. These developments, however, are noteworthy and point out the consequences of three decades of armed insurgency. As the PKK evolved, so did the society it claimed to represent and defend. Tactics, ideology, framing, and discourses all changed along with the world and the reality in which the insurgents operated. The outcomes of such a remarkable transformation, the sociopolitical changes that have arisen out of this decades-long struggle, are what this book attempts to explore. Below I first outline a short history of the PKK,[10] followed by the chief social and political consequences this insurgency has engendered over the course of three decades.

The PKK in Brief

During the formative years of modern Turkey (1923–1938), the Kurds failed to forge a state of their own or to redefine their relationship with the Turkish state. This produced a long, coerced tranquility in the Kurdish East. While a number of Kurdish organizations peacefully occupied the political arena throughout the 1960s and 1970s, the rise of the PKK in the late 1970s, along with subsequent armed conflict in 1984, disrupted the outward calm. The government responded by deploying hundreds of thousands of regular troops and special operations forces to the region. The armed conflict peaked in the early 1990s and to date has generated nearly fifty thousand deaths. Following the capture of the PKK's leader, Abdullah Ocalan, in 1999, the PKK announced a unilateral ceasefire and sought a negotiated peace settlement with the Turkish government.

While some progress was made in addressing the restive Kurdish minority's grievances in the early 2000s, there was general dissatisfaction with the pace and depth of reforms (Gurses 2010). Furthermore, the U.S. invasion of Iraq in 2003 strengthened the ten-year-old Kurdish autonomous region in the North and created opportunities for the PKK to attack Turkish targets across the border. The result was sporadic yet intense armed clashes between the PKK and Turkish armed forces. Ultimately, the unilateral ceasefire came to an end and the death toll quickly reached 167 in 2004, climbing to 349 deaths in 2008. The transborder linkages among the Kurds who live in Syria and Turkey coupled with the onset of civil war in Syria in 2011 complicated the conflict in Turkey. Clashes between the Turkish military and the PKK intensified, resulting in at least 541 casualties in 2012 (Tezcur 2014; Gurses 2015a).

In December 2012, in a renewed effort to resolve the conflict peacefully, the governing Justice and Development Party (Adalet ve Kalkinma

Partisi, AKP) initiated talks with the PKK's jailed leader Ocalan. These talks, in contrast to the PKK's earlier unilateral ceasefires, resulted in a period of calm that was largely observed by both Turkey and the PKK. The ceasefire that began in early 2013, which many hoped would be a prelude to comprehensive peace negotiations, came to an end in July 2015. This has resulted in the bloodiest and most destructive phase of the three-decade rebellion. Intensification of the armed conflict, with the Turkish army laying siege to several Kurdish cities and towns, has produced thousands of casualties as well as widespread destruction of buildings and property, and alleged Turkish military abuses.[11] The surge in violence has ended the peace process and rekindled fears that armed conflict may engulf the entire society and become a full-blown civil war between the two peoples.

Whether the protagonists will answer the calls for negotiating peace has yet to be seen, but the conflict that started in 1984 and peaked in the mid-1990s has had profound effects on the socioeconomic and political fabric of the society. The three-decades-long armed conflict has generated tens of thousands of deaths, ravaged the economy in the Kurdish region, and resulted in a migration of internally displaced rural Kurds to major Turkish cities and beyond.

The Evolving Insurgency

The PKK's evolution started when it parted ways with the Turkish leftist movement, morphing into more of a secessionist socialist organization. With its roots in the Turkish leftist movement of the 1970s, the PKK was formed in 1978 as a clandestine organization with the initial intention of establishing an independent, socialist Kurdish state. This goal was later replaced by "democratic autonomy" aimed at seeking solutions within the existing frame of Turkey. The classical Marxist notions of "class struggle" and "historical materialism" were progressively replaced by such terms as "individual emancipation," "humanization," and "self-production" in the second half of the 1990s (Grojean 2008; also see White 2015). With a focus on developing a pluralist, grassroots-driven democracy, new concepts such as "democratic confederalism" and "ecological democracy" were introduced to adapt to the changing environment in the post-2000 era (Ocalan 2011; for a summary see Leverink 2015).

Since its formation in the 1970s, the PKK has shown a remarkable ability to navigate between the complex and overlapping events of "social movement" and "revolution," the ultimate goal of which ranges from a policy change to overthrowing the state (see, for instance, Goldstone 1998). While traversing between "revolution" and "social movement," the PKK has, for the most part, acted like a revolutionary movement by violently challenging the regime. At other times, however, it has denounced violence and sought reconciliation with the Turkish state.

The PKK's remarkable transformation resembles Charles Tilly's metaphor of repertoires as "claim-making routines." Tilly (2008, 14), a leading authority on social movements and contentious politics, compares the process of claim making to "jazz and commedia dell'arte rather than ritual reading of scripture." Drawing attention to both the learned and improvisational character of claim making, he concludes that "like a jazz trio or an improvising theater group, people who participate in contentious politics normally have several pieces they can play, but not an infinity. . . . Within that limited array, the players choose which pieces they will perform here and now, and in what order."

The PKK's motive for violence has been in line with the "learned" and "improvisational" character of claim-making routines. The group has primarily been reformist in using violence against the state. Despite its initial goal and the rhetoric of a united socialist Kurdish state, the group has in practice sought to redefine its relationship with existing institutions. It is nonetheless revolutionary in its relationship with the Kurdish society in that it pursues a substantial overhaul in the values, norms, institutions, and circumstances that facilitate or hinder its desired sociopolitical objectives, a process Gurr (1973, 362, 384) calls social change.

Although violence has remained a part of its "repertoire of contention" (Tilly 2008), the insurgency has engendered a number of nonviolent organizations at both the local and national levels. Akin to what McCarthy and Zald (1977, 1219) call the "social movement industry," the PKK insurrection has given rise to a number of political organizations including the Democratic Society Congress (Demokratik Toplum Kongresi, DTK), the Democratic Regions Party (Demokratik Bolgeler Partisi, DBP), and the Peoples' Democratic Party (Haklarin Demokratik Partisi, HDP).

The DTK, an umbrella organization for pro-Kurdish groups, "is not simply another organization, but part of the attempt to forge a new political paradigm, defined by the direct and continual exercise of the people's power through village, town and city councils" (Akkaya and Jongerden 2014, 193). The DBP commands great presence in local governance in the Kurdish-dominated East, and its sister party, the HDP, has been successful in receiving support from millions of Kurds as well as a minority of Turkish liberals and leftists who lent their support in an effort to check the excessive power of the ruling AKP.

The insurgency has also stimulated a number of women's groups with radical feminist agendas and laid the groundwork for local committees to be formed and for women to effectively participate in their affairs (Acik 2014; White 2015; Gurses 2016). It is worthwhile to note that this grassroots-based sociopolitical paradigm is not only advocated by the pro-Kurdish political parties in Turkey but has also been an inspiration for the aforementioned PYD of Syria to create inclusive local assemblies in parts of the country under its control (Drwish 2016). Thus the social and political changes that the PKK has brought about have the potential to influence the sociopolitical dynamics of rapidly changing Syria and Iraq.

Outcome Variables

What is social and political change? Clearly, these concepts are multidimensional and difficult to define and quantify. I find the following definition provided by Gurr (1973, 362) useful in studying the effects of war on social change: "any collective change in the means or ends of human action," referring to changes in people's values, norms, situations, or institutions by which they organize or are organized for action.

In my application of the term "political culture," following Wood (2003, 219), I refer to attitudes toward different institutions as well as norms of group solidarity and collective identity. Wood's emphasis on "collective identity," defined as "an individual's cognitive, moral, and emotional connection with a broader community," is particularly pertinent in describing the changes in political culture of Kurds as a result of violent conflict.

With a focus on violence committed against noncombatants, I look into the anatomy of a civil war and seek to explore several central questions regarding the social and political legacies of conflict at the micro level. More specifically, do wartime experiences engender positive attitudes toward women? Does exposure to conflict-related violence help forge an engaged citizenry and lay the groundwork for a democratic culture at the micro level? How does civil war help forge a national identity? Does a war between groups that hail from the same faith impact minority groups' relationships with the common faith? Can conflict dynamics facilitate a secularization process?

Plan of the Book

In the process of searching for answers to these complicated and multifaceted issues, I build on the growing literature targeting the transforming effects of civil war on civilian populations. Civil war kills and maims people, destroys the environment, disrupts economic production, and results in massive population displacements. The case studied here is no different. Part I demonstrates the destructive nature of war, ranging from the physical destruction to an array of psychosocial problems, and then to the detrimental effects of war on the environment. I document the dark side of conflict in chapter 1.

In part II, I offer an alternative, integrated theory of war and change that emphasizes the contextual nature of civil war violence along with its consequences. After summarizing divergent explanations and findings on the civil-war-change spectrum, I present an analytical framework that lays out the mechanisms through which social and political changes occur (chapter 2).

Despite the horrific aspects of war, evidence suggests that civil war as a complex event is likely to generate multilayered outcomes. In part III, I analyze these outcomes and examine how exposure to violence during civil war forces active and passive participants to re-examine their value systems. Civil war not only destroys lives and property but also dismantles the patriarchal social structure prevalent in most war-torn countries. Chapter 3 assesses the effects of war on creating new opportunities for women. It addresses the contingent nature of violent conflict and the changing roles of and attitudes toward women.

In chapter 4, I discuss the impact of war on political culture. Examining the democratizing potential of civil war, I argue that the war-democracy nexus is not limited to the macro level. Just as war dynamics have been shown to be associated with postwar democratization at the country level (Wood 2000, 2001; Wantchekon 2004; Gurses and Mason 2008; Joshi 2010; Huang 2016), wartime experiences also engender a democratic political culture at the individual level. Armed conflict often helps articulate social, economic, and political grievances in a society and paves the way for the rise of an activist identity. Next, this chapter examines the connection between war and nation building and its effects on creating a sense of belonging and a common consciousness that makes up an important part of political culture defined above.

In chapter 5, I examine the complicated relationship between civil war and religion. Significantly, this chapter tackles the secularizing potential of ethnic armed conflicts that involve ethnic groups hailing from the same faith. I argue that ethnic conflict between coreligionists (as in the case of Muslim Kurds versus a government dominated by Muslim Turks) undermines religious ties and reinforces ethnic identities among members of minority group, leading to the rise of a national identity in which religion plays a subordinate role.

In part IV, I turn to the prospects for peace building. Chapter 6 discusses "the way forward" in light of the theories and observations presented in the first three sections. Building on the negative and positive changes of civil war previously discussed, this chapter considers the prospects for a lasting peace in an increasingly divided country and unstable region. I conclude with a summary of the argument and findings.

Research Design

To examine the multilayered outcomes of civil war, this book employs two main approaches. First, I draw on an original survey that documents individual war experiences from the Kurdish conflict in Turkey. The dataset consists of responses from randomly selected individuals from Diyarbakir, Van, and Sanliurfa, three major Kurdish-populated provinces in Turkey. These provinces were selected to represent the Kurdish-populated regions' diversity in terms of socioeconomic development, varying degrees of Kurdish ethnic concentration, and exposure to violent conflict.

Diyarbakir and Van provinces are known for their strong support for the PKK insurgency and pro-Kurdish political parties. These two provinces have been a primary site of the armed conflict between Kurdish rebels and the government and have become destinations for tens of thousands of internally displaced people from the countryside. Sanliurfa province is distinguished from Diyarbakir and Van by its heterogeneous ethnic composition that includes a significant Arab minority and support for center-right political parties. The pro-Kurdish political parties, despite making some inroads in the province, have not been able to win the greater municipality mayoral race in Sanliurfa. In the local elections of March 2014 the governing AKP scored a landslide electoral victory, while the pro-Kurdish Peace and Democracy Party (BDP), the predecessor of the aforementioned HDP, won approximately one-third of the total votes. Moreover, Sanliurfa, partly because of a geography unconducive to guerrilla warfare, has remained on the sidelines of the armed conflict that has greatly influenced the daily lives of ordinary citizens in Diyarbakir and Van.

Diyarbakir province has seventeen districts (*ilce*) with each district divided into dozens of smaller units (*mahalle*). These *ilce* and *mahalle* show an important variation. Study participants were selected using a multistage stratified cluster sampling with age and gender quotas applied to obtain a representative sample. Stratification was both appropriate and necessary because in all three provinces certain neighborhoods are known for their strong support for the insurgency and contain many internally displaced families. Baglar district in Diyarbakir, for instance, is a geographical area with frequent violent protests and clashes with the police; however, with its thirty-five *mahalle* and a population of more than 350,000 people, Baglar also displays significant variation. Thus, to ensure that each cluster is adequately represented, with probability proportional to population size, a total of ninety-two clusters (*mahalle*) were selected in Diyarbakir province: thirty-eight in the city of Diyarbakir and the remaining fifty-four from the thirteen rural districts. Participants were then randomly selected from these strata using comprehensive phone directories produced by major telecommunication service providers in the country. A similar strategy was followed to obtain samples from the other two provinces.

The survey was administered by Roni Research, a public-opinion research company based in Istanbul, between June and September 2014.[12] This professional public-opinion company has branches in the Kurdish-dominated provinces. Local teams[13] in each province were employed to carry out the survey. Upon obtaining participants' consent, members of the research teams met with the participants at their homes or at a location of their choice. The research teams conducted 700[14] face-to-face interviews that lasted about forty-five minutes from each of these three provinces, resulting in a total of 2,100 interviews.[15]

Civil war violence can take different forms: direct, indirect, physical, and nonphysical (Kalyvas 2006; Balcells 2010, 2012).[16] Exposure to violence, the central explanatory variable in this study, includes participants' experiences with the arrest, torture, or death of a family member as well as displacement because of the armed conflict. The responses show a high degree of exposure to violence; nearly half of the participants indicated they were exposed. This number for Diyarbakir, as a primary site of the armed conflict, was higher than that of Van and Sanliurfa (57 percent, 45 percent, and 33 percent, respectively).

Nearly 30 percent of the respondents stated that they know someone who was the victim of torture, 31 percent stated that they know someone who abandoned their home, while 12 percent said they fled because of the conflict. The data also shows that 14 percent lost a family member, 12 percent were arrested, and 8 percent were tortured.[17]

These numbers are in line with findings from another study conducted in 2010. According to this nationwide survey, which also included Diyarbakir and Sanliurfa along with three other Kurdish-dominated provinces, 13.5 percent of the respondents that resided in Kurdish-populated provinces abandoned their homes and about 18 percent had a family member who died or was wounded because of the conflict (KONDA 2010). Thus, notwithstanding concerns and questions regarding survey data, these statistics confirm the assumption made earlier about a high prevalence rate and provide evidence for the sample's representativeness.

Clearly, the survey data provides a snapshot of changes the war has engendered. While the overall picture out of this large sample of 2,100 individuals is revealing, it might fail to capture the longitudinal aspect of the changes described here. These developments are likely to be a result of wartime traumas acquiring meaning during protracted conflicts and turning those traumas into valuable experiences from which significant sociopolitical changes arise. To provide further evidence for the mechanisms through which exposure to violence during civil war facilitates a cultural change, I conducted in-depth face-to-face interviews with dozens of individuals whose lives were affected by the armed conflict. These lengthy interviews help infer valid causal inferences between key explanatory and outcome variables. The interviews took place over a few years, during which I took several field trips to Turkey, Canada, and Belgium.[18]

Interviewees were selected through nonrandom purposeful and snowball sampling[19] of a diverse group of people that included ex-combatants; civilians who were detained, tortured, or forced to flee their homes for their suspected links to the PKK; family members of PKK militants/supporters who sought refugee status in Canada and Belgium; and many others who have never been arrested, yet grew up in the conflict zone. I contacted pro-Kurdish political parties' local branches in the Kurdish region of Turkey to identify individuals who have been displaced or exposed to other forms of violence. I also relied on personal contacts to conduct face-to-face in-depth interviews with selected individuals and families at their homes. This enabled me to better observe changes in attitudes as well as behavior toward women. In Canada and Belgium, I primarily relied on Kurdish associations in these countries to identify potential interviewees.

As already mentioned, the primary focus of this book is to contribute to the literature on how wartime experiences facilitate sociopolitical change. In joining others (e.g., Tripp 2015; Huang 2016), the arguments advanced in this study are aimed at enhancing our understanding of the war-change spectrum. They are not meant to glorify, promote, or condone violence. Using the case of the PKK in Turkey, an unlikely candidate for such change, I aim to provide a comprehensive analysis of the war-change connection. The questions addressed in this book are not of academic significance alone. This is a particularly pertinent question at present, given the division of the Kurds between four countries of great geostrategic importance and the dramatic changes taking place in the region.

PART I

## ONE

The Dark Side of War

Civil war has replaced interstate conflict as the most frequent and destructive form of warfare in the post–World War II era (Eriksson, Wallenstteen, and Sollenberg 2003; Fearon and Laitin 2003). Civil conflicts have caused millions of casualties, destroyed infrastructure, disrupted production and trade, threatened external markets (Collier 1999; Bayer and Rupert 2004; Murdoch and Sandler 2004; Kang and Meernik 2005), generated environmental degradation (Etten et al. 2008; Brauer 2009; Rueveny, O'Keef, and Li 2010; Gurses 2012), and forced many from their homes (Collier et al. 2003; Moore and Shellman 2004).

In addition to these direct and immediate consequences, scholars have also pointed out indirect and long-term effects of civil war. In a cross-national analysis, Ghobara, Huth, and Russet (2003) identify lingering effects of civil war on public health and conclude that conflict is especially harmful to women and children. Iqbal (2006) reaches a similar conclusion that conflict undermines public health through damaging infrastructure, interrupting access to basic services, and disrupting agricultural production.

Chamarbagwala and Moran (2011, 43), utilizing data from Guatemala's thirty-six-year civil war (1960–96), examine the impact of the conflict on education and find that internal armed conflict has detrimental effects on human capital accumulation for the most vulnerable demographic groups, rural Mayan males and females. Lai and Thyne (2007, 289), using cross-sectional time series data for all states between 1980 and 1997, demonstrate that "civil wars are likely to reduce educational expenditures as well as educational enrollments across all levels."

A range of psychosocial problems, including suicide, alcoholism, post-traumatic stress disorder, sleep disorders, child neglect, and overwhelming feelings of hopelessness as a result of exposure to violence, have been identified in numerous countries such as Afghanistan (Scholte et al. 2004), Cambodia (Sack, Clarke, and Seeley 1996), Rwanda (Pham, Weinstein, and Longman 2004), Sri Lanka (Somasundaram 1998), and Israel (Palmieri et al. 2010).

The case studied here is no exception. In addition to the human costs associated with the PKK insurrection in Turkey, which at the time of this writing had produced about fifty thousand deaths,[1] the Turkish state's counterinsurgency measures, particularly the forced evacuation of more than three thousand villages in the Kurdish countryside during the mid-1990s, resulted in a massive population displacement (Jongerden 2007). According to one account nearly two million people were uprooted by 1995 because of this conflict (Cohen and Deng 1998, 48). By the end of the 1990s, this number was estimated to be around four million (Jongerden 2001; McDowall 2004). A report by the International Crisis Group cites at least 2,798 confirmed deaths between July 20, 2015, and May 14, 2017.[2] This surge in violence since July 2015 has also resulted in more than 350,000 internally displaced persons and massive urban destruction in some southeastern districts (Mandiraci 2016).

These numbers might at first glance seem to be proportionally low when compared to other conflicts. For example, according to a report by Human Rights Watch, five decades of conflict between the Revolutionary Armed Forces of Colombia (Fuerzas Armadas Revolucionarias de Colombia, FARC) and successive Colombian governments has forcibly displaced nearly six million people, amounting to 13 percent of the total population and generating the world's second largest population of internally displaced persons (IDPs).[3] In El Salvador, the twelve-year civil war (1980–92) took nearly 2 percent of the total population and displaced another 10 percent (Wood 2003, 2008).

In contrast to these cases, the Kurdish conflict, due mainly to its ethnic character, has been primarily confined to the Kurdish-dominated eastern regions of Turkey. Estimating the exact human costs of the conflict thus requires controlling for this geographical and demographic aspect. The total population of twenty-five provinces that hosted the conflict or were impacted by it in one form or another was about seventeen million people as of 2015.[4] Thus, four million IDPs constitute approximately 25 percent of the total population of seventeen million. In other words, the three decades of armed conflict has displaced about a quarter of civilians in the East. It should be noted that some of these provinces (i.e., Erzurum, Kilis, Malatya, and Gaziantep) are neither Kurdish-majority provinces nor did they become a site of armed conflict in the 1990s. Excluding them increases the proportion of Kurdish civilians uprooted from their homes by the conflict to 30 percent.

These statistics are confirmed by the rapid urbanization many Kurdish cities experienced in the 1990s. Gurses (2012), based on the census data, reports that the conflict generated a massive wave of internally displaced Kurds heading to major cities in the region and beyond. Between 1990 and 2000, the city population of Diyarbakir increased by 38 percent. Batman, another province with a high rate of armed clashes between the state forces and the PKK, experienced a 57 percent increase. Sirnak, a smaller province with rough terrain that borders Iraq and Syria, saw a 69 percent increase in its city population for the same period. The city population of Hakkari, a mountainous province bordering Iraq on the south and Iran on the east, increased by 96 percent.

During the same period, Ankara, the nation's capital and second largest city, saw an increase of 25 percent in its city population. Even more strikingly, the city population of Istanbul, the single largest city in the country and one that has historically been an attractive destination for millions, went up by 34.5 percent for the same period; this rate is about one-third of what Hakkari had for the same years (see table 1). It is important to stress that Kurds, the majority of whom were forced out of their homes in the 1990s, make up an estimated 10 percent of total population in Istanbul. Internally displaced Kurds also account for sizable portions of urban population growth in other major Turkish cities such as Adana, Mersin, Izmir, and Bursa.

While a multitude of factors play a role in forced migration in a civil war context (Adhikari 2013), the deliberate depopulation of the countryside constituted a key aspect of Turkish counterinsurgency measures directed at isolating the insurgency. These measures also resulted in detrimental

TABLE 1. Armed Conflict, Internal Displacement, and Urbanization, 1990–2000

Province	City Population (1990)	City Population (2000)	% Change
Diyarbakir	600,640	817,692	36
Batman	193,621	304,166	57
Sirnak	125,264	211,328	69
Hakkari	71,099	139,455	96
Ankara	2,836,719	3,540,522	25
Istanbul	6,753,929	9,085,599	34.5

effects on the environment in which the conflict occurred. As Etten et al. (2008) note, in the Kurdish case the depopulation of the Kurdish countryside and deforestation were neither the product of the state's economic development plan nor a result of state inability to enforce its authority in the Kurdish countryside. Instead, they were direct results of the state's policies of containing the PKK insurgency by cutting rebels off from their logistic support base and eliminating their natural shelter.

As a part of this counterinsurgency plan, state forces undertook a systematic practice of burning forests, which resulted in a measurable deforestation of the Kurdish region. Etten et al. (2008) report that somewhere between 7.5 percent and 25 percent of all forests in the province of Tunceli, which became a site of heavy fighting in the 1990s, were burned down as part of this strategy. Bingol, another province that saw intense fighting between Turkish forces and PKK rebels, saw a 68 percent decline in its productive forest area between 1984 and 2005 (Gurses 2012). The use of total population of forest villages as a proxy for deforestation confirms the conflict's detrimental effects on forests. The total population of forest villages for the two provinces noted above declined by 51 percent and 25 percent, respectively, between 1990 and 2000 (Gurses 2012).

The forced relocation of the Kurdish rural population has also negatively impacted agriculture and animal production that form a substantial part of the region's economy. Utilizing data from the province of Tunceli, Etten et al. (2008) show that between 1990 and 1995 the province lost 25 percent of its crop cultivation area and saw a significant reduction in the size of herds; Tunceli lost 58 percent of its sheep, 67 percent of its goats, and 51 percent of its cattle herds. Diyarbakir, the largest province in the region, lost more than half of its sheep and goats in the 1990s (Gurses 2012).

The conflict has also generated indirect yet long-lasting negative effects on public health and education. Similar to studies that have pointed out damages that civil conflict inflicts upon societies, Kibris and Metternich (2016), utilizing yearly data on public health in Turkey between 1964 and 2010, demonstrate that the conflict in Turkey has exerted long-term negative influences on public health by driving medical personnel away from conflict regions. Another study examines the adverse effects of the conflict in Turkey on the educational achievement of high school students. Kibris (2015), using the test scores of more than 1.6 million high school students who took the nationwide University Entrance Exam in 2005, finds that students from the conflict zone fell significantly behind.

This negative side of the conflict is not limited to effects that are relatively easy to define and measure. Before presenting statistical evidence for the dark side of the conflict, another painful but more subtle aspect of the conflict merits attention. That is the nearly impossible task of identifying if, where, and when many Kurdish young men and women fell. Over the course of more than three decades of armed conflict, tens of thousands of Kurds have lost their lives, which has turned the Kurdish countryside into a graveyard.

The locations of the remains of thousands of Kurds or the circumstances under which they died are often unknown. While the PKK has been making an effort to keep records of its militants after 2000, records for those died in the 1990s, which arguably bear witness to the heaviest fighting, are nonexistent or not reliable. Even for those with available records, the best the families can expect to receive is a "confirmation" of the death of their loved ones. Families often prepare a funeral ceremony and set up a tent to receive condolences, sometimes years after their son's or daughter's death.

In addition, since the September 12, 1980 military coup, but peaking in the 1990s, hundreds of Kurdish civilians have been declared "lost under custody." The dead bodies of some of these "disappeared" were later found tortured and deserted. Some were never seen or heard from again. Inspired by the Mothers of Plaza de Mayo in Argentina, a group of mothers of the disappeared initiated a silent protest movement in Istanbul in 1995. This vigil, which has come to be known as the Saturday Mothers (Cumartesi Anneleri), includes dozens of Kurdish mothers of the disappeared, who gather every Saturday at noon in front of the five-hundred-year old Galatasaray High School in Istanbul to protest the disappearance of their children under police custody (Arifcan 1997; Baydar and Ivegen 2006). Not knowing the fate of their children or having their remains has resulted in chronic grief, traumatic stress, and generalized anxiety (Yuksel and Olgun-Ozpolat 2004).

Moreover, during my fieldwork over the past several years, increased drug use among youth, previously unknown to the conservative Kurdish society, and a rise in burglaries and break-ins were among the two most common complaints from locals in the city of Diyarbakir. Suicide among women, especially teenage girls, has been on the rise in the past decade, another tragic outcome that is often ascribed to conflict-related traumas.[5]

An Empirical Look at the Dark Side of the Conflict

Survey data collected in 2014 reinforce conclusions about the negative consequences of the conflict. In line with studies that have pointed out psychosocial problems associated with conflict, those who are exposed to violence tend to show lower levels of interpersonal trust, appear to be "less satisfied" with their lives, and overall are less "hopeful" about the future.

As noted earlier, the central explanatory variable, exposure to violence, was constructed using responses to a set of questions aimed at identifying participants' experiences with the arrest, torture, or death of a family member, as well as displacement because of the armed conflict. To come up with a cumulative measure of exposure to violence, following Bellows and Miguel (2009), I created a victimization index by taking the average of responses to the conflict-related questions presented in table 2. This overall measure of exposure to violence ranges from 0 to 1 with a mean of .18 and a standard deviation of .25.

The "interpersonal trust" was measured using data on participants' responses to "Would you say that people are generally trustworthy, somewhat trustworthy, not very trustworthy, or untrustworthy," with responses based on values ranging from "untrustworthy" (1), "not very trustworthy" (2), "somewhat trustworthy" (3), and "very trustworthy" (4). Responses to the statement "Overall, I am very satisfied with my life," that take values

TABLE 2. Descriptive Statistics for Independent Variables

Variable	Min	Max	Mean	Std. Deviation
Exposure to Violence Index	0	1	.18	.25
Have you ever been arrested because of the conflict? (Yes/No)	0	1	.12	.33
Have you ever been tortured because of the conflict? (Yes/No)	0	1	.08	.27
Have you ever abandoned your home because of the conflict? (Yes/No)	0	1	.12	.32
Have you lost a family member or close relative because of the conflict? (Yes/No)	0	1	.15	.35
Has anyone in your family or anyone you know had to take refuge or abandon their home because of the conflict? (Yes/No)	0	1	.31	.46
Has anyone in your family or anyone you know been the victim of torture because of the conflict? (Yes/No)	0	1	.29	.45
Control Variables				
Sex (0 = Male; 1 = Female)	0	1	.35	.48
Age	1	5	3.03	1.08
Education	1	5	2.94	.98
Automobile (Yes/No)	0	1	.53	.50
Children	0	14	3.06	2.55
Religiosity	1	4	3.51	.66

ranging from "strongly disagree" (1), "disagree" (2), "agree" (3), to "strongly agree" (4) were used to assess the overall impact of conflict on respondents' satisfaction levels. To examine the link between conflict and being hopeful about the future, I utilized responses to "How hopeful are you about the future?," which takes values from "not at all hopeful" (1), "not hopeful" (2), "rather hopeful" (3), to "very hopeful" (4).

The findings confirm the negative effects of conflict reported in the existing literature. For example, similar to what Rohner, Thoenig, and Zilibotti (2013; also see Grosjean 2014) found in their examination of the 2002–2005 conflict in Uganda, war exposure seems to have a negative and significant effect on respondents' subjective evaluation of how trustworthy people are. As demonstrated in model 1 of table 3, exposure to violence is associated with lower interpersonal trust.

Model 2 of table 3 shows results for the effect of conflict exposure on participants' satisfaction with their lives. The negative coefficient on the primary explanatory variable indicates "less satisfaction" or less agreement with the statement that "Overall, I am very satisfied with my life." Likewise, findings reported in model 3 suggest a dampening effect of conflict

TABLE 3. The Dark Side of Violent Conflict: Trust, Life Satisfaction, and Hope

Variable	Model 1 (Trust)	% Change	Model 2 (Satisfied)	% Change	Model 3 (Hope)	% Change
Exposure to Violence	-1.52***	-31	-2.15***	-.41	-.91***	-20
Index	[.18]		[.20]		[.20]	
Sex	.03	1.7	-.22**	-10.2	-26***	-12
	[.09]		[.10]		[.10]	
Age	.09*	11.1	.20***	25.2	.08	9
	[.05]		[.06]		[.06]	
Education	.07	7.8	.03	3.7	.16***	17.1
	[.05]		[.06]		[.06]	
Automobile	-.10	-5	.31***	16.8	.11	5.9
	[.09]		[.10]		[.09]	
# of Children	.04	11.1	-.08***	-19.2	.05*	13.8
	[.02]		[.03]		[.02]	
Religiosity	-.09	-6.3	.37***	28.2	.34***	25
	[.07]		[.07]		[.07]	
Cut 1	-3.31		-2.88		-2.17	
Cut 2	-.07		.37		.64	
Cut 3	4.86		4.7		4.57	
N	2100		2100		2100	
Pseudo R^2	.02		.06		.02	
Prob > Chi^2	<.0001		<.0001		<.0001	

Note: * significant at 10 percent level; *** significant at 1 percent level (two-tailed). Robust standard errors in brackets.

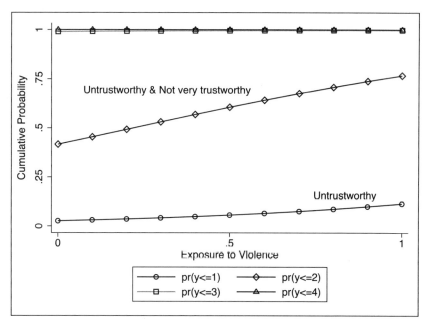

Figure 1. Conflict and trust toward others

on being hopeful about the future. These effects hold even after controlling for the effects of a range of socioeconomic and demographic variables
summarized in the lower part of table 2.

The results presented in table 3 are obtained using an ordered logistic
regression. Due to the nonlinear nature of the models, I provide odds ratios
to interpret these findings. As shown in column 3, one standard deviation
increase in the value of the exposure to violence index decreases the odds
of agreeing with the statement used to gauge trust toward others by 31 percent; it results in an even greater decline of 41 percent in life satisfaction
(column 5); and makes participants less hopeful by 20 percent (column 7).

These findings are also illustrated in figures 1 through 3. The cumulative probability of "untrustworthy" and "not very trustworthy" shows a
noticeable increase as the exposure to violence index rises (figure 1). The
negative effect of conflict on life satisfaction is even more noticeable. As
presented in figure 2, the cumulative probability of "strongly disagree"
(SD) and "disagree" (D) with the statement that "Overall, I am very satisfied with my life" shows a substantial increase as a result of an increase in
the exposure to violence index. Finally, while the effect of conflict on feel-

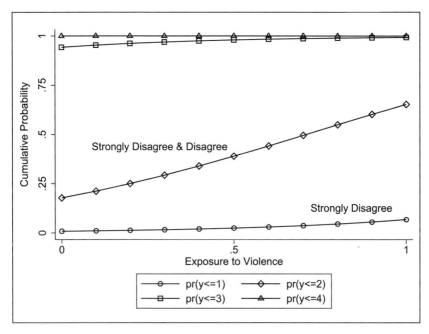

Figure 2. Conflict and life satisfaction

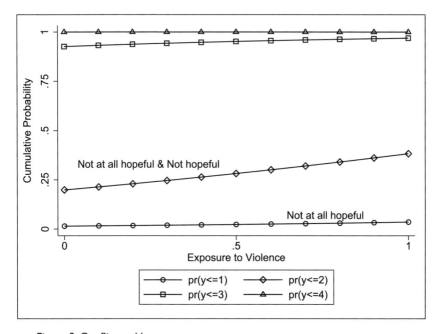

Figure 3. Conflict and hope

ing less hopeful is not as blatant as the effect on life satisfaction, it nonetheless is discernible, as demonstrated in figure 3.

Nonetheless, despite these negative physical and psychosocial effects, the overall picture that emerges out of conflict shows that "continuing personal distress and growth often coexist" (Tedeschi and Calhoun 2004, 2). I will elaborate on this "other" side of the war in the next chapter and outline the mechanisms through which war brings about positive sociopolitical changes.

PART II

## TWO

Toward an Integrated Theory of Civil War and Change

Despite evidence for the disastrous consequences of conflict described in the previous chapter, scholars from multiple disciplines have pointed out positive outcomes of civil war. Discussing positive aspects of war, one group of scholars draws attention to war's potential for change and examines the impact of war at the macro level. Cramer (2006, 282), pointing to the violent beginnings of capitalism, notes that "war combines destruction with change." He (2006, 10) challenges the argument that war is simply a "development in reverse" (Collier et al. 2003) and argues that violent conflict can have progressive outcomes as it carries the seed of societal creativity and reform.

Chafe (1999, 30), drawing on the role World War II played in producing massive changes, notes that war is not only "a time of anxiety and fear" but also "a moment of possibility." He argues that the wartime mobilization helped transform American society; it ended the Great Depression, paved the way for the next thirty years of economic development, and generated "a sense of possibility and optimism for the first time in a generation" for the two most marginalized groups in the United States, women and blacks. Grosjean (2014), using data from a representative survey of 39,500 individuals in thirty-five countries, examines the link between wartime experiences and sociopolitical preferences. She concludes that exposure to wartime violence is not only associated with the erosion of social and political trust but also stimulates collective action.

A growing body of research has pointed to the democratizing potential of civil war. Armed conflict, these studies argue, can create opportunities for balanced power relations through the redistribution of economic and political powers among the contending forces, and thus facilitate democratization after the war (Wood 2000, 2001; Wantchekon 2004; Gurses and Mason 2008; Joshi 2010; Armey and McNab 2015).

Turning to the micro-legacies of civil war, much of the existing literature scrutinizes the effect of traumatic wartime experiences on generating social and political changes at the individual level. These studies argue that war transforms participants' outlooks on life by disrupting traditional norms and values, breaking the barrier of fear, and bringing up hidden strengths. As traditional ways of life—often characterized by political quietism, deference to authority, and patriarchal power arrangements—come under attack, subjects undergo a cultural change and acquire new roles and skills to cope with new circumstances.

Voors et al. (2012), building on the case of Burundi, argue that exposure to conflict spurs a shift in preferences and results in displaying more altruistic behavior toward neighbors. Wood (2003) and Gilligan, Pasquale, and Samii (2013) demonstrate respectively that victimization by war-related violence resulted in greater collective action in El Salvador and Nepal. Bellows and Miguel (2009) draw attention to increased political participation in Sierra Leone, while Blattman (2009) points out a substantial increase in political engagement in Uganda. Tripp (2000, 2015) provides an extensive analysis of how war engendered new possibilities for Ugandan women.

To explore the resultant sociopolitical changes at the individual level, several studies draw from psychological literature on personal growth after traumatic events (e.g., Bellows and Miguel 2009; Blattman 2009; Voors et al. 2012). This argument, which has come to be known as "posttraumatic growth theory," posits that tragic events can result in a process from which victims "derive meaning, feel wiser, and face uncertain futures with more confidence" (Tedeschi and Calhoun 1996, 469). Reflective of this argument, Pearlman (2016) argues that the Syrian civil war has created opportunities for self-expression and a need to overcome fear that has become a seminormalized way of life. Bateson (2012) goes further still, pointing to crime victimization as a key factor behind increased political participation. Building on a cross-national analysis, she points to expressive reasons such as the need to redefine and reaffirm their identities to explain why crime victims tend to become more engaged in civic and political life.

This social-psychological approach is mainly consistent with studies by psychiatrists who point out positive outcomes of war despite its obvious destructive nature. An early work (Glover 1935, 135) describes war as a dramatic attempt to solve some difficulty that provides a positive outlet for unconscious destructive desires. Volkan (1979, 241) argues that war reduces collective aggression, turns passivity into assertion, and increases self-esteem in order to compensate for the pain and suffering that the process engenders. Somasundaram (1998, 226–27), drawing on the civil war in Sri Lanka, points out how war brings up hidden strengths and leadership skills and results in breaking up caste systems and class barriers.

The theoretical underpinnings of the nexus between war and change in much of the existing literature are largely based on the contention that exposure to conflict produces positive outcomes through changes often associated with posttraumatic growth. Wartime experiences *as* traumas can lead to changes in self-perception, interpersonal relationships, and a changed philosophy of life, three broadly perceived benefits associated with posttraumatic personal growth (Tedeschi and Calhoun 1996, 456). This approach treats social and political outcomes of war as a given and fails to distinguish between civil war traumas and those due mainly to non-political circumstances. Implicit in this premise is that victimization during civil war is essentially equivalent to crime victimization or experiencing a major life crisis.

From a psychoanalytical perspective, trauma is often associated with disbelief, disorientation, and difficulty in comprehending the situation. While the word trauma refers to an injury inflicted on a body, in psychiatric literature it is often used to describe a wound inflicted upon the mind that results in the breach in the mind's experience of time, self, and the world (Caruth 1996, 3–4). Thus the condition of being traumatized involves "the incapacity to respond adequately to a terrible and shattering event" and, equally important, the inability to "make meaning from the ruins of experience" (Britzman 2000, 33). As Philipose (2007, 62) summarizes, "trauma is the experience of a world unmade and undone."

While the posttraumatic growth theory is useful in exploring the effect of violence as a trauma, not all traumas are of the same nature. Growth after a personal tragedy or positive outcomes of "volunteerism, community spirit and social consciousness" reported after natural disasters (Glencorse and Shakya 2015) are different from the type of social and political changes born of protracted civil wars. Therefore this thesis, which was developed by clinical psychologists to explain growth after highly challenging life crises—such as rape, cancer, HIV infection, or heart attacks (Tedeschi and Calhoun 1996; 2004)—might fail to capture the complex and contextual nature of violence during civil war. Experiences of a rape victim or cancer survivor, for instance, are qualitatively different from incentives, dynamics, and processes involved in a conscious decision to lend support to rebels and thus become a victim of state violence.

The terms "victim" and "trauma" may not even be appropriate to describe the suffering and pain in a civil war context. These emotions reimagined and reinterpreted in an environment often characterized by resentment, discontent, and repression change the nature of violence and its consequences. This aspect of the conflict environment defies the definition of trauma provided above (the incapacity to make sense of the situation). Thus a heavy reliance on this approach runs the risk of "depoliticizing" a phenomenon that is by definition political and context-dependent. In other words, it discounts the "inherent complexity" and "messiness" of civil war (Kalyvas 2006, 392). Political motives are particularly salient in the context of civil war and greatly influence both macro-level dynamics as well as local dynamics (Balcells 2017, 43).

As Keen (2005, 289) argues, a civil war (even one characterized by notoriously brutal violence such as the conflict in Sierra Leone) cannot be reduced to "a collapse of reason, a collective lapse into evil and irrationality," despite the horrendous atrocities committed against civilians and the role of economic agendas that at times blurred the line between "war" and "crime." Drawing attention to social and psychological context that gave rise to greed and atrocity, Keen concludes that the Sierra Leone conflict in the 1990s should not be confined to a struggle for power and diamonds. It was also driven by social exclusion and the absence of avenues for communication, or by the "assertion of power by powerless."

Another group of studies by and large ascribe improvements in women's rights to the disruptions brought by wartime. These works reason that patriarchal networks and gender roles can be radically altered during war as women take on unprecedented roles as combatants, interlocutors with authority, mediators, or heads of household. These new roles for women help break down social, political, and economic barriers, lead to an expansion of women's public roles and responsibilities, blur the line between private and public spheres, and result in the questioning of conventional gender roles (Mason 1992; Blumberg 2001; Karam 2001; Wood 2008; Kaufman and Williams 2010; Menon and Rodgers 2015).

While war creates incentives and opportunities for different roles and responsibilities, developing coping mechanisms may not necessarily translate into social and political change. Participants will engage in all sorts of activities and behave differently to survive or even benefit from a war. The ongoing Yemeni civil war between a Houthi-led movement and progovernment forces since 2014 has had devastating humanitarian consequences yet has also become "the mother of reinvention." Consistent with the argument that the exigencies of war create opportunities for participants to devise coping strategies, many Yemenis have resorted to solar panels as an alternative source of energy in the midst of collapsing state authority and failing services (Fahim 2016).

While wartime experiences help challenge conventional gender roles and responsibilities by blurring the line between women's private and public roles, it is qualitatively different than adopting a solar panel. Managing the immediate demands of a conflict environment or learning how to cope with wartime realities may not necessarily lead to sociopolitical changes.

This failure to distinguish between different types of exposure to violence, along with researchers taking wartime experiences out of context, has produced conflicting findings over the link between this variable and its purported outcomes. The lack of clearly specified causal mechanisms has resulted in a pessimistic view of the effects of war on gender relations. Studies have pointed to the superficial, temporary, and transient nature of the expansion of women's roles and responsibilities during civil war. Wartime activism or attitudes, some have argued, may not necessarily constitute a social change or carry over in a postwar environment. Women might find themselves sidelined, pushed out of public life, or made to suffer backlash against newfound freedoms once the constraints of war are lifted (Ahmed 1982; Pankhurst 2003; Viterna 2014). Similarly, while several studies highlight a substantial increase in political engagement and participation arising from violent conflict, others point out consequences such as political extremism and hostility toward minorities (Canetti-Nisim et al. 2009), along with hardening attitudes toward rival out-group members (Grossman, Manekin, and Miodownik 2015).

Therefore the relationship between exposure to violence during civil war and its consequences should be qualified. The experiences of an individual who is caught in the crossfire, or who stands to benefit from the war, or of those who are racketeering amidst the chaotic war environment are qualitatively different than the experiences of those carrying their scars as a badge of honor. For example, members of a progovernment militia or "village guards"—a paramilitary force made up of Kurds allying with the government against the PKK in return for material gain—will have fundamentally different views of violence than the Kurds who refused to enlist in these paramilitary armed guards and were coerced to leave their homes.

An alternative approach to the unmediated effects of violent conflict, inspired largely by women's empowerment in postwar Uganda, draws attention to a number of domestic and global factors as facilitators in the gains in women's rights. While postconflict trajectory is found to have a significant and independent effect on women's rights (Hughes and Tripp 2015), the positive changes that postconflict countries in Africa have experienced are conditioned by the strength of prior domestic women's mobilization (Tripp 2000) or changes in international gender norms primarily after 1995 (Tripp 2015).

Another study echoing mechanisms identified by Tripp (2000)—i.e., the potential of conflict to disrupt the social, political, and economic fabric of a society—underscores the conflict dynamics as a key to changes in postgenocide Rwanda. To explain the positive changes that have resulted in a parliament with the highest number of women in the world, this study lists two additional factors that facilitated the change: solidarity and partnership with women's organizations and a political leadership that created a favorable environment for women's promotion (Uvuza 2014, 197).

These extensive analyses throw considerable light on women's changing roles as a function of war. More importantly, the stress on mediating factors serves as an important reminder for the need to contextualize violence during civil war. Still, these studies examine cases that ended in decisive rebel victories whose victors introduced measures that benefited women. Absent territorial control during the war and a decisive military victory for the rebels, these changes might not have occurred.

Such an analysis focuses mostly on changes at the country level with an emphasis on such areas as political representation and women-friendly policies and legislation. It is plausible that changes in international norms (mainly after the end of the Cold War when many countries, including those emerging from destructive civil wars, experienced notable democratization) may have played an important role in producing social and political change. Feminist-leaning legislation (such as the introduction of quotas in government for women) imposed from the top down might have been prompted by factors ranging from political leadership to changes in international norms and disruptions in traditional gender roles and responsibilities because of the war. Such a fusion, however, makes it difficult to empirically ascertain the impact of war violence on the outcome.

Having sketched the existing perspectives and their shortcomings, I now present a framework to specify the context-dependent aspect of wartime violence. Civil wars do not occur in a vacuum; studying the effects of wartime experiences thus entails several contextual variables that could fundamentally change the social and political outcomes of war. Specifically, I show how exposure to violence during civil war is contingent upon the framing of violence in producing social and political change as defined in the introduction. I attempt to fill an important gap in the existing literature on the conditional effect of violent conflict. The hypothesized positive effects, I argue, are largely a function of how wartime suffering and experiences are interpreted or framed.

Violence in a Context

Earlier works ascribe violent conflict to sociopolitical environments characterized by resentment, discontent, and repression (Davies 1962; Gurr 1970) or to social strains that cause a "disequilibrium" from which the desire for revolutionary change arises (Smelser 1963; Johnson 1964). Violence, as Hannah Arendt (1969, 69) argues, is neither beastly nor irrational. Rather it occurs when one's sense of justice is offended. It helps emphasize grievances and brings them to public attention, despite the risk of the means becoming the ends themselves.

Although the frustration-anger-aggression principle constitutes the basis of relative deprivation theories, there is more to consider. As one prominent scholar of this approach notes, while it is essential to analyze "the minds of men and women who oppose bad governments and unpopular policies," there is also a need to "know about the societies in which they live, their beliefs and cultural traditions, and the governments they oppose" (Gurr 2012, 281). In other words, while "grievances" and "sense of injustice" help explain the genesis of a fertile ground for revolution that induces political action, the context under which these developments occur can greatly shape not only the prospects of violent conflict but also its social and political consequences.

Seeing collective actions through explicitly political prisms, proponents of resource mobilization theory highlight the critical role leadership and organization plays in framing and manipulating grievances and discontent (McCarthy and Zald 1977; McAdam, Tarrow, and Tilly 1996). In other words, the outrage and displeasure that relative deprivation theory deems as the culprit behind inducing a revolutionary state of mind can "be defined, created, and manipulated" in the hands of political entrepreneurs (McCarthy and Zald 1977, 1215).

Just as grievances can be manufactured or manipulated, so can the suffering and pain that accompany civil war. The history of the transforming aspect of pain and its enduring legacy, which has been subject of countless philosophical, religious, psychological, and literary works, is as old as the pain itself. Franz Kafka (1949, 209) writes in his diaries, "Accept your symptoms, don't complain of them; immerse yourself in your suffering." The novelist Milan Kundera (1991, 200) describes suffering as "the most fundamental of all feelings" and assigns a bigger role to it than thought in forming the self.

The German philosopher Friedrich Nietzsche speaks of suffering as a necessary, even desirable, force for growth and self-development (Brogan 1988). In explaining the role it plays in the process of suffering becoming strength, Nietzsche highlights the significance of "meaning" and "purpose." Only when these questions of "suffering for what?" or "why do I suffer?" are sufficiently answered, he argues, do positive outcomes arrive. In his words, man "in the main was a *sickly* animal: but suffering itself was *not* his problem, instead, the fact that there was no answer to the question he screamed, 'Suffering for *what*?' Man, the bravest animal and most prone to suffer, does not deny suffering as such: he *wills* it, he even seeks it out, provided he is shown a *meaning* for it, a *purpose* of suffering" (Nietzsche 2006, 28, italics in original).

Echoing the Nietzschean approach to suffering, the psychiatrist Viktor Frankl underscores the significance of adding meaning and depth to suffering. Frankl (1985, 162, 170), drawing on his own experiences in Nazi concentration camps, argues that suffering can be turned into something positive and constructive. Changing attitudes toward unavoidable suffering may trigger a process from which sufferers acquire the capability to cope with suffering and turn it into a transformative experience. This ability to ascribe new meaning to a personal tragedy may result in turning suffering into accomplishment with a change in worldview and an incentive to take responsible action.

An insurgency is not limited to violence alone to accomplish its goals. Insurgents will utilize all available resources and make use of pre-existing social networks to harness antigovernment feelings in framing their struggle for "justice and equality." In an effort to broaden their base and win over the population they claim to represent and fight for, a rebel group needs to offer an alternative explanation for the frustration, pain, and suffering the conflict brings upon the civilian population. Clearly, this could not be accomplished by waging a guerrilla war alone. Dissident leaders must also answer the question of "*why* do I suffer?" for those subjected to war.

An insurgent organization can be treated as a social movement organization (SMO) that represents and shapes the broadly held preferences, opinions, and beliefs in a population that desires a change in some parts of social structure (McCarthy and Zald 1977, 1217). In articulating, manufacturing, or manipulating shared grievances, an insurgent group may adopt violent as well as nonviolent actions to reach its target goals. For example the aforementioned nonviolent political organizations inspired by the PKK insurgency, including the DTK and DBP, as well as a number of women's groups, all share the common goal of representing the yearning for justice shared by a large portion of Kurds and of remedying the unequal relationship Kurds have with the state. This multipronged approach to attain a set of goals is analogous to what McCarthy and Zald (1977, 1219) call "social movement industry" (SMI).

The effects of wartime experiences will thus be largely conditioned by an insurgency's capacity as an "industry" to portray real or perceived injustices within the system and, more importantly, by its ability to attribute them to the state. Insurgencies as SMIs are actively engaged in the production of meaning for supporters, bystanders, observers, and antagonists (Benford and Snow 2000). Through their words, actions, and ideologies, rebel leaders attempt to shape reality for their potential supporters. As Chong (1991, 165) argues, success in large-scale political activism addressing such issues as civil rights and peace is primarily shaped by the leadership and organization that could muster the community resources and enlist the aid of outside allies. The very nature of exposure to violent conflict can be radically changed when the threat of going to prison no longer serves as a deterrent but rather is taken as a badge of honor (Chong 1991, 82). Pain and suffering seen through this prism can be transformative and lead to "a progressive practice of empowerment" (Tønder 2013, 6).

But the purported effects vary greatly within members of a minority group engaged in an armed conflict with the state. As noted earlier, violent conflict will have different effects on those caught in the crossfire than on those committed to the cause of insurrection. Irrespective of the strength of the insurgent network or SMI, its support base will include elements ranging from "constituents," who provide resources for insurgency, to "adherents," who believe in the goals of the movement, and to "bystander public," whose involvement is limited to witnessing insurgent activity. Of course, there will also be "opponents" who do not adhere to rebels' narratives and goals (McCarthy and Zald 1977, 1221). The latter group, from rebels' perspective, generally consists of "collaborators," such as members of the progovernment "village guards" mentioned above. As Kalyvas (2006, 98) notes, despite heterogeneous individual motivations ranging from security and the desire for social standing, to economic concerns involved in joining progovernment militias, ideology or commitment to the cause is not a primary factor. This factor, which is largely missing in current literature, has important implications for the war-change nexus. Different motivations and justifications will have different consequences.

Similarly, the asymmetric nature of many civil wars, which often involve states that enjoy military superiority relative to the insurgents, suggests that wartime experiences are different for the groups involved. Security imperatives and related justification processes are likely to fail to produce the purported outcomes for members of the dominant group. The effect of war on members of the dominant group claiming to represent the state as a "coercion-wielding organization" (Tilly 1990, 1) that legitimately monopolizes the use of physical force (Weber 1946, 78) is qualitatively different than the effect on those who rebel in the name of "justice."[1]

Results from a study that examined reactions to the loss of young adults support this conclusion. Yuksel and Olgun-Ozpolat (2004) divided ninety participants who had lost their first-degree relatives in the previous five years into three groups. The first group includes relatives of soldiers who died in the conflict between the PKK and Turkey (group I); the second was composed of relatives of the mostly Kurdish disappeared persons, some of whom formed themselves into the protest organization of Saturday Mothers noted in chapter 1 (group II); and relatives of young people who died of leukemia at the University Hospital in Istanbul made up the third group (group III).

The researchers found that although all participants were diagnosed with at least one mental problem, those who lost relatives to the conflict (groups I and II) had higher chronic grief and traumatic stress when compared to those who lost relatives to leukemia (group III). And the severity of the psychiatric illness was found to be higher among those whose relatives had died in military service (group I).

Moreover, in line with the argument made above that wartime experiences affect sufferers differently, the researchers point out an important difference between subjects in groups I and II. The Kurdish mothers ascribed meaning to their loss and interpreted the deaths as part of a wider context through which their children acquired a new identity, whereas the mothers of Turkish soldiers had difficult times making sense of their losses despite the state-sanctioned elevated status of martyrdom and social and financial privileges that often accompany the death of soldiers. It is worth noting that at their six hundredth vigil on September 24, 2016, a group of the Saturday Mothers (from which group II was selected) renewed their calls for those responsible to be held accountable but also expressed the desire for "peace and justice" so that no one else would have to suffer their fate.[2]

This qualification helps explain conflicting findings on the effect of exposure to violence in the existing literature. While some studies found that violent conflict has resulted in greater political engagement or the development of altruistic attitudes toward neighbors, others, based upon the Israeli-Palestinian case, point to how combat exposure hardens attitudes toward the rival (Grossman, Manekin, and Miodownik 2015) or leads to exclusionary political attitudes among those personally exposed to violent conflict (Canetti-Nisim et al. 2009). Kibris (2011), using the Kurdish conflict in Turkey, reaches a similar conclusion. Analyzing the effect of Turkish security forces casualties on the electoral outcomes in Turkey in the 1991 and 1995 general elections, she finds that such an exposure makes the Turkish voters "less concessionist," which leads to an increase in the vote share of right-wing Turkish parties with more intransigent positions on the issue.

Outlining Mechanisms of Change

In light of these arguments, I advance four main mechanisms through which wartime experiences lead to change. *First*, violence during civil war tends to be particularly brutal and "intimate," involving "a record of closeness and peaceful interaction between victims and victimizers" (Kalyvas 2006, 11). Exposure to violent conflict could personalize the war by provoking emotions and feelings and helping develop and strengthen righteous impulses. Violent conflict and the ensuing suffering may comfort the sufferers by helping them to connect on a special level of mutual understanding and make them particularly empathetic toward the disadvantaged groups. This could lead to a situation what Tønder (2013, 6) calls "empowering pain" from which a strong will and desire to grow arises.

Moreover, new opportunities and roles created during the war may help break down social, political, and economic barriers and lead to changes in social relations and hierarchy. These unmediated linkages constitute the essence of much of the existing literature that draws on the psychology of personal growth after traumatic events or emphasizes disruptions that wartime creates in producing sociopolitical changes.

Nonetheless, there is a need to distinguish between those personally exposed to violence and "bystanders" who merely observed violence. As others have demonstrated, civil war violence is not only of strategic nature but also can take various forms (Kalyvas 2006; Balcells 2010, 2012, 2017). Noncombatant participants could be exposed to wartime violence directly in the form of arrest, torture, or forced migration. They could also experience it vicariously, such as through the loss of a friend or family member. Due to different logics and processes involved, direct or "intimate" violence is more likely to provoke the type of emotions and feelings that could lead to a change in social and political culture.

Second, war "is a transformative phenomenon" and it "transforms individual preferences, choices, behavior, and identities" mainly through violence (Kalyvas 2006, 389). In the process, violence changes character; it is qualified for individuals caught up in war dynamics. Wartime experiences and violence gain meaning through insurgent ideologies that may help frame suffering, assign meaning to it, and offer an alternative vision to those who suffer. As active signifying agents, insurgent leaders engage in the production of meaning, which has been referred to as "the politics of signification" (Hall 1982, 64).

In addition to this direct link, an effect that is likely to be limited to those with certain political sophistication, ideology can also have a more subtle effect on the outcome by creating or conditioning the atmosphere for "framing" suffering. Ideology can provide individuals with a proper language to express their anger, frustration, and desires.[3] Although, as Gutierrez-Sanin and Wood (2014) have argued, while explanations based on economic interests or situational logic have come to dominate works on civil war, an insurgent group's political ideology as a program of action that works as a blueprint that guides and regulates insurgent group's behavior is essential in understanding variation in violent patterns.

The type of ideology adds an important qualification to the war-change nexus; it shapes violence and its potential consequences. Ideology can slow or accelerate political development by deterring or facilitating the shift in values toward change. An ideology that enforces and celebrates women's liberation will condition wartime violence differently than the one that relegates women to a secondary class. For example, the ideology of the aforementioned IS, a group responsible for much of the recent human misery and atrocity in Syria and Iraq, closely resembles what Freire (2000, 37) calls sectarianism that "mythicizes and thereby alienates." The interaction of such a dogmatic ideology that insulated itself against change with violence may not be transformative. It is rather "castrating" and obstructive as it "turns reality into a false (and therefore unchangeable) 'reality.'" While violence might be of strategic value for the IS, its victims are likely to struggle with the "meaning" of the situation, making trauma rather than growth a likely outcome.

Not coincidentally, some of the most intensely studied cases in which current literature focuses on positive outcomes of war are those with egalitarian, often leftist ideologies. Neil Sheehan (1988, 171), in his *A Bright Shining Lie*, compares the communist Viet Minh to several competing nationalist factions in North Vietnam. Sheehan concludes that the non-communists failed because they lacked the interest in social change necessary to mobilize people. The communists survived mainly "because their concern with social goals always took them back to the bottom, where there was discontent on which to build."

Huang (2016), drawing attention to wartime origins of postwar democratization, examines a list of all major civil wars that started and ended between 1950 and 2006 and concludes that rebels' reliance on civilians is a significant predictor of postwar democratization. Statistical tests also lend some support for wars that involved rebel groups espousing Marxist ideology followed by greater democratization. While Huang cautions that this finding needs further scrutiny, she also reasons that it is a likely consequence of several characteristics of Marxist rebels: they tend to rely more on civilian support than non-Marxist rebels, are often led by highly educated leaders and emphasize literacy among civilian supporters; and they encourage women's participation in their struggle.

Alison (2004, 460), in her examination of women's participation in ethnonationalist armed groups in Sri Lanka and Northern Ireland, concludes that "different contexts produce different gender construction." Significantly, she finds that women have been much less involved in loyalist, pro-state paramilitaries in Northern Ireland than in the antistate Irish Republican Army that conceives of itself as "liberatory."

Another study, using a global sample of rebel organizations active between 1979 and 2009, investigates the variation in women's deployment in combat roles. It concludes that rebel groups' political ideology greatly explains the extent of women's participation in war. Specifically, "Marxist and other leftist insurgencies employ the highest numbers of female fighters while an Islamist ideology substantially depresses the proportion of female fighters within rebel organizations" (Wood and Thomas 2017, 43–44).

The *third* mechanism involves what others have described as the educational aspect of mass mobilization. The liberating facet in this context refers to actors seeing history as a possibility or something that can be transformed. Learning occurs as participants re-create the way they see themselves and enter the historical process not as objects but as responsible subjects (Freire 2000, 36). In the words of a former PKK combatant, who fought eleven years in the ranks of the insurgency, "my experiences as a guerrilla taught me that there is always a way, that I can bring about change."[4]

Analyzing the relationship between the oppressed and oppressor, Freire (2000, 46–47) points to the "fear of freedom" as an obstacle to be overcome. Liberation not only requires overcoming the fear of repression but also "the fear of freedom." The latter requires ejecting the image imposed by the oppressor and replacing it with autonomy and responsibility. Gultan Kisanak, the first female comayor of the Kurdish city of Diyarbakir, who was tortured and kept in a dog hut for six months for refusing to renounce her Kurdish identity in a notorious Diyarbakir prison in the 1980s, notes, "my life in prison" helped me "destroy fear" and "develop self-confidence" (Kisanak, Al-Ali, and Tas 2016).

Studies of the American civil rights movement have identified similar gains. Button (1989, 241), in a study of the impact of the civil rights movement on the real-life situations of southern blacks, draws attention to "a sense of racial pride, confidence, and cohesiveness" that the movement engendered in black political culture in the South. Another study points out that this liberating aspect of participation was not only for the blacks but also for the whites who stood by them. Newfield (1966, 40–41) notes that "the sit-ins clearly liberated more white middle class students in the North than it did Southern negroes" as students at northern campuses began "to realize that a jail record could be a badge of honor." Chong (1991, 78) argues that participation could spur a sense of mastery over society and could educate about the competing interests of that society and the workings of the political process, thus leading to personal growth even if the designated purpose of public action is unfulfilled. Wartime experiences can thus lead to what Harold Lasswell (1951, 473) calls "rectitude," a sense of responsibility that is intrinsic to democratic character.

While this mechanism suggests a direct linkage, as with the second mechanism, leadership's success in holding the state responsible and developing a language that participants can use in relating their experiences to the context of war dynamics is likely to play a key role in producing change. Kisanak, the above mentioned comayor of Diyarbakir, also underlines the significance of leadership and ideology in framing the struggle, or findings an answer to "suffering for *what?*"

The *fourth* mechanism differs from the previous ones in that it is more pertinent to a subcategory of civil wars, those that involve groups fighting to reconfigure ethnic relations. These wars include ethnic challengers that are at odds with the identity of a state, who seek to redefine or divide the state itself, or who strive for major changes in their relationship with the state (Sambanis 2001, 261–62). These conflicts are often characterized as particularly intractable, involving fighters that are largely mobilized along ethnic or religious lines with the ultimate goal of obtaining some form of autonomy or outright secession (Kaufmann 1996; Horowitz 2000).

Civil war violence, unlike state repression or genocide, is not unilateral. It is characterized by its strategic use and produced by at least two actors competing over governing the population rather than exterminating it (Kalyvas 2006, 31). As such, civil war bears a resemblance to the sixteenth-century European state-making processes that involved violent conflict or "sequences of demand, resistance, and control" (Tilly 1975, 23). This aspect is emphatically present in the secessionist or ethnonationalist insurgencies described above. Such insurgencies face unique challenges as they ideally seek to go beyond waging an armed conflict alone and carve out a state of their own. They also aspire for both domestic and international recognition as the legitimate and able representative of the minority they claim to fight for (Stewart 2015).

While ethnonationalist rebel groups, as the rival claimants to sovereignty, hope to build a state through extracting resources from the population and presenting themselves as the legitimate representatives of their people, they also pursue conflict to forge a national identity with which members of the warring group could identify. Although state making and nation building involve several overlapping processes that may appear simultaneously or in different orders, they are not the same. In Finer's (1975, 88) words, these two processes have "historical and logical connections" but the latter emphasizes a process by which a community attains a common consciousness. State making involves "the works of combining, consolidating, neutralizing, manipulating a tough, complicated, and well-set web of political relations" during which protagonists "face a furious resistance" while trying to "dissolve large parts of the web" (Tilly 1975, 25). Whereas, struggle for nation building occurs more at the societal level and is directed at forming "a community of feeling . . . based on self-consciousness of a common nationality" (Finer 1975, 86).

Similar to what Hobsbawm (1983, 1–3) argues with regard to the role of "invented traditions" to establish social cohesion and instill certain values and norms, insurgent leaders and organizations not only utilize pre-existing social networks to mobilize potential supporters for the war but also strive to create continuity with a real or artificial past. Pointing out the paradoxical nature of trauma, Hutchison (2016, 3) argues that trauma can both break and construct political communities. The traumatic aspect of civil war and the histories it creates can result in collective forms of meaning and bring those "affected" together around the shared pain and suffering.

Aydin and Emrence (2015, 130), drawing attention to such an aspect of civil wars as "group-making projects," argue that while insurgencies fight for identities that already exist, they also aim at building new ones. Tilly (2002, xi), with a focus on the role of stories in political mobilization and conflict, pinpoints political identity stories as "collective, public replies to the question 'Who are you?'" Stories in this context are treated as outcomes of contentious politics. While stories can fuel the war efforts, the war also (re)creates stories, songs, sagas, and heroes to inspire and educate, all of which contribute to developing a sense of common destiny, a belonging that constitutes a key aspect of the nation-building process. War can thus help forge a national identity, leading to a significant change in the political culture of participants as defined earlier.

This mechanism of war as a nation-building force also has consequences for the secularization potential of civil war, an aspect that is almost entirely missing in the current literature.[5] This is partly because the cases on which the majority of these studies are based do not easily lend themselves to such an analysis. In El Salvador, a case studied extensively by Wood (2000, 2001, 2003) and Viterna (2014), both the rebels and government shared the same faith yet the insurgents were not at odds over the ethnic identity of the state; rather the war was fought over the apparatus of the state.

In the decade-long Sierra Leone conflict of the 1990s, ethnic and religious divisions did not play a central role (Bellows and Miguel 2009). Despite ethnic divisions, national politics often cut across ethnic lines; class and ethnicity do not necessarily coincide in Sierra Leone (Keen 2005, 46). The main rebel group, the Revolutionary United Front (RUF), was an ethnically mixed group and targeted people from every ethnicity (Richards 1995). The Angolan civil war of 1975–2002 was fought primarily in the context of the Cold War. It began as a proxy conflict between the ruling People's Movement for the Liberation of Angola (MPLA), which was supported by the Soviet Union and Cuba, and the National Union for the Total Independence of Angola (UNITA) backed by the United States and South Africa. The ethnic aspects of the conflict were pronounced only after the Cold War dimensions dissipated (Tripp 2015, 117).

The NRA in Uganda, another case that has been the subject of several studies examining both political and social outcomes of civil war, was not a narrow ethnic organization in spite of the ethnic dimensions involved. The group's leadership was largely from the Ankole province in southwestern Uganda, whereas most of the fighting took place in the Buganda-inhabited region to the north of Kampala (Lyons 2016, 1030). In Rwanda, where ethnicity played a much more prominent role, the rebels did not seek to carve

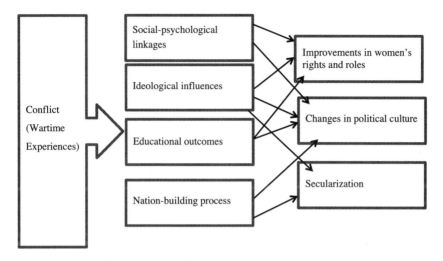

Figure 4. Wartime experiences and sociopolitical change

out an independent state of their own. In this respect, it resembles the conflict in El Salvador, where the primary goal of the rebels was to overthrow the regime. These contrast with the ethnic conflict examined here.

In the context of civil war, religion often becomes a part of the political arsenal to sustain the fight. As religion itself is turned into a contested field, warring parties are likely to interpret religion in a way that serves their political interests. Religion is then bound to be redefined and re-examined, leading to multiple contending interpretations. This politicization of religion, particularly in cases where a warring ethnic minority challenges a government dominated by coreligionists, results in relegating religion to a subsidiary role. Thus the armed conflict, coupled with the politicization of religion that turns religion into an instrument to bolster the warring groups' agendas, reinforces ethnic identity at the expense of religious identity.

This secularization potential of civil war constitutes an important part of the social as well as political change described in this study. Conflict forces participants to re-evaluate the role of religion in their lives, which may lead to changes in norms, values, and behavior. It also contributes to the rise of some type of a "national church" that could facilitate forging a distinct national identity in which common faith no longer serves as a bond that ties coreligionists to one another.

The secularization argument laid out in this book, however, applies more to ethnonationalist groups who are often secessionist in their goals and desires or who seek autonomy in one form or another. Furthermore, consistent with the context-dependent, political nature of civil war, this linkage is provisional; it relates to cases in which rebels and dominant ethnicity hail from a common faith. Schematically, these linkages are summarized in figure 4.

These channels constitute the building blocks of change in social (most notably, changes in women's roles and responsibilities and shifts in attitudes toward women) and political (developing an activist culture, forging a national identity, and secularization as an integral part of the nation-building process) culture. Wartime experiences may help develop a sense of righteousness, create new opportunities for women, strengthen the bonds between members of the group that facilitate the rise of a national identity, and result in a significant decline in religion's role and place in national and individual identities. In the next section, I elaborate on these four mechanisms and demonstrate how they apply to the Kurdish conflict in Turkey.

PART III

THREE

War and Women

A growing number of women began to join the PKK in the late 1980s and early 1990s; according to one estimate they made up one-third of new recruits by 1993 (Marcus 2007, 173). This significant increase in women's membership resulted in noteworthy changes to women's roles and positions within the Kurdish movement. Today, women are a substantial part of the insurgency, making up some 40 percent of PKK guerrilla units and functioning in all levels of decision making.[1] Women have become an integral part of the organizations and parties formed or inspired by the PKK movement. They have been elected as mayors, parliamentarians, and cochairs. Below, I delineate the primary mechanisms through which these changes have occurred. The analysis shows that gains in women's rights have mostly been a result of a combination of a progressive ideology and war dynamics.

Since its inception in 1978, the PKK has described itself as a modern and revolutionary force for change committed to eliminating traditional structures of sociopolitical organization (Jongerden and Akkaya 2011). Over the past four decades the PKK has parted ways with the Turkish left and acquired a more "Kurdish" identity that transcends regional, tribal, religious, and class divisions within Kurdish society. It has also strived for going beyond what the PKK leader Ocalan calls "primitive nationalism," a narrow form of nationalism often associated with traditional Kurdish groups and movements.[2]

Kurdish movements' search for universalism through mainly leftist ideologies precedes the rise of the PKK (H. Bozarslan 2017). In the

1960s a number of Kurdish groups in Turkey resorted to a socialist discourse by portraying Kurdistan as a "colony" and Kurds as a "colonized people." Viewing national oppression and economic exploitation of the Kurds through these prisms gained widespread acceptance among Kurdish activists from the 1970s onwards (Gunes 2013, 250). It was the rise of the PKK in the 1980s, however, that led to a convergence of leftist ideals and Kurdish nationalism to an unprecedented degree. In the words of Hamit Bozarslan (2017), a renowned Kurdish studies scholar, the PKK redefined Marxism-Leninism with a high dose of Fanonism, emphasizing the creation of decolonized human beings through resistance. The PKK leader Ocalan, describing Kurdish history as one of enslavement, called for violent resistance to liberate Kurdistan and, more importantly, to free Kurds from their interiorized enslavement.

The search for universalism, through a hybrid of Marxist-Leninist discourse and a newly adopted framework inspired in part by the writings of American political theorist Murray Bookchin, has given rise to such concepts as "democratic autonomy" and "ecological democracy," with an emphasis on pluralist, grassroots-driven local administrative units and radical gender equality.[3] Described by its leader as a social revolution and uprising against the old social order, the PKK has aimed at transforming Kurdish identity and creating the New Man (Grojean 2008, 4). The emphasis on gender equality that constitutes a chief tenet of the PKK's vision of social change should be considered within this context.[4]

Women's participation in Kurdish rebellions did not start with the PKK. As Bengio (2016, 31) notes, "Kurdish history is replete with cases of charismatic women assuming leadership roles in the religious, political and military spheres." But these women were small in number and consisted mainly of wives, daughters, and relatives of leading figures. With the rise of the PKK in the late 1970s and the ensuing armed conflict in the 1980s, gender issues became a key aspect of Kurdish rebellion. One key feature that separates the PKK from earlier rebellions is its successful mass mobilization of women and the subsequent break with traditional gender roles (Caglayan 2012).

As noted earlier, despite an unfavorable environment characterized by a conservative Islamic culture, low levels of socioeconomic development, and limited prior domestic women's mobilization, women have become an integral element in the Kurdish movement. They have moved from eligible to aspirants to candidates and from candidates to elected officials (Sahin-Mencutek 2016). The push for women's representation and women's social and political empowerment has been transformative for both the movement and for women. It has produced significant positive changes in a region sometimes referred to as "the patriarchal belt" characterized by strict control over women's behavior (Caglayan 2012).

The struggle for gender equality within the Kurdish movement can be observed on multiple fronts. In the legal arena (*legal alan*), Kurdish political parties inspired by (or accused by the state of being extensions of) the PKK became the first political institutions in Turkish history to introduce a voluntary quota for women to overcome the barrier to entry. In 1999 the Kurdish People's Democracy Party (Halkin Demokrasi Partisi, HADEP) set a 25 percent quota for women to redress gender imbalances in the composition of all intraparty structures, including both elected and nonelected assemblies. The PKK leader Ocalan's push to increase the gender quota coupled with war dynamics that empowered Kurdish women resulted in increasing the quota for women from 25 percent to 40 percent in 2005 (Kisanak, Al-Ali, and Tas 2016; Sahin-Mencutek 2016).

These policies have yielded serious results. Of the thirty-seven mayoral races won by the HADEP in the Kurdish-dominated region in the 1999 local elections, three were won by women candidates. The number of female mayors from the Kurdish political party increased to fourteen in the 2004 local elections. A decade later, in the 2014 mayoral elections, the Kurdish Peace and Democracy Party (Baris ve Demokrasi Partisi, BDP) had more female mayors (twenty-three) than the governing AKP (six), the main opposition Republican People's Party (Cumhuriyet Halk Partisi, CHP) (six), and the far-right Turkish Nationalist Action Party (Milliyetci Hareket Partisi, MHP) (one), combined.[5]

Similarly, in the 2007 national legislative elections, eight female candidates, making up 36 percent of the total seats gained by the Kurdish Democratic Society Party[6] (Demokratik Toplum Partisi, DTP), were elected to the national parliament. This trend continued in the 2011 national elections; 34 percent of the total parliamentarians elected to the Grand National Assembly of Turkey on the Kurdish BDP's[7] ticket were women. In the June 7, 2015, general elections, the pro-Kurdish Peoples' Democratic Party (Halklarin Demokratik Partisi, HDP) won eighty seats in the Turkish National Assembly, 39 percent of which were women (Kisanak, Al-Ali, and Tas 2016; Sahin-Mencutek 2016).

In the illegal front (*illegal alan*), the PKK's Fifth Congress of 1995 is often cited as a watershed meeting since it addressed several long-standing important issues. The PKK leadership made a strong critique of the Soviet approach to socialism, pointing out its pan-Russian chauvinism, extreme centralism, and decline in individual freedom as the main causes of Soviet-era stagnation. The leadership emphasized the need to create a new militant identity that with great care, understanding, and resolve seeks to overcome all difficulties, a militant that turns the negative into something positive and, stressing the diversity and richness of Kurdistan and the Middle East, calls for cooperation between all disadvantaged groups. This idea would later give birth to the concepts of "democratic autonomy" and "democratic confederalism," with an emphasis on community-based, pluralist democratic coexistence within the existing framework of nation-states.

Significantly, the Fifth Congress formalized the growing number and power of Kurdish women within the insurgent movement by establishing a separate, independent women's army, the Kurdistan Free Women's Union (Yekitiya Azadiya Jinen Kurdistan, YAJK) (Tax 2016a, 119–30).[8] This is not unique to the PKK. Nations as diverse as El Salvador, Sri Lanka, and Nepal have witnessed a similar phenomenon: "unprecedented numbers of women have left their homes, picked up guns, and defied cultural norms to quite literally fight for revolutionary change" (Viterna 2014, 4). The establishment of a separate women's unit was not, however, merely a result of the need to increase the number of fighters. Instead, the YAJK (which later became YJA-Star)[9] was a reflection of the changes the war dynamics had brought about as well as the result of an ideological commitment to empowering women and changing both men and women with regard to gender and gender equality. In other words, the transformation of gender relations was not a sidebar to the PKK but rather was considered to be a central task that would ultimately determine the success or failure of the entire endeavor (Tax 2016a, 128).[10]

This commitment to gender equality as part of creating a new society grew stronger over time. The PKK leader Ocalan (2013, 9) would later describe "the 5000-year-old history of civilization" as "essentially the history of the enslavement of woman." He (2013, 11) portrays women as the first "slaves," the first subjugated group: "the enslavement of men comes after the enslavement of women. Gender enslavement . . . is attained through refined and intense repression combined with lies that play on emotions. Woman's biological difference is used as justification for her enslavement. . . . Her presence in public sphere is claimed to be prohibited by religion, morally shameful; progressively, she is secluded from all important social activities." Ocalan is unwavering about women's role and place in the PKK and the struggle for freedom by which new identities are created. Calling for a "total divorce" from the five thousand years of male domination, he has spoken of the need to "kill the male" and described the PKK as a "party of women."

This discourse and underlying ideology equates women with nature, as portrayed in the ideal matriarchal society of ancient Mesopotamia. It successfully integrates gender issues into the Kurdish national struggle for a radically redefined relationship with the dominant, oppressive groups. Despite the risks involved in blending gender issues with nationalist agendas (Cockburn 2007), Kurdish women's participation on both nationalist and feminist fronts has been described as complementary, promoting and feeding one another (Bengio 2016).[11]

Even though the changes fall short of the ideal picture portrayed by the PKK leader, they call attention to the significance of ideology in producing these positive outcomes. Sebahat Tuncel, a female member of parliament for the Kurdish Peace and Democracy Party (BDP), a predecessor of the HDP, describes the issue as a double-edged sword. While referring to Sakine Cansiz's (a female founding member of the PKK) contribution to the movement, Tuncel argued that "while we fight to end the unequal treatment of the Kurds in Turkey, as women we also fight another battle, the male dominance within the Kurdish society" (Butler 2013).

The conflict environment enabled Kurdish women to criticize the way their own sex was used as a basis for discrimination by men in the movement. Kisanak, the first female comayor of Diyarbakir, highlights challenges in overcoming entrenched patriarchal tradition within Kurdish society. She argues that, akin to justifications used in other cases, women's issues were sidelined based on the pretext that the time was not ripe for such changes. In her own words, "this is not something we were given. We had to fight for every single advance" (Kisanak, Al-Ali, and Tas 2016). Accounting for the gains in women's rights, Kisanak draws attention to wartime experiences, changes in international norms, and women's struggles against the patriarchal culture and practices within the Kurdish society and movement. Notably, she underlines the significance of the leadership and ideology in improvements in women's rights.

A thirty-six-year old female interviewee, a former high school teacher who had recently immigrated to Canada, pointed out that "war dynamics created conditions for Kurdish women to discover their true potential, helped them question the unequal gender roles, and demand change in their status in the society." She also highlighted a key difference between earlier Kurdish rebellions and the PKK insurgency: the latter shows important differences in its approach to gender equality. She concluded that war dynamics are only one factor in changes in gender relations that the Kurdish society has experienced. Without "a strong commitment to gender related issues," she asserted, these "positive outcomes" may not have been achieved.

Another interviewee drew attention to a certain segment of the Kurdish community in Toronto, which he described as "traditional," "patriarchal," even "backward" despite their support for the Kurdish political movement. In explaining this outcome, he pointed out that the part of the Kurdish region they emigrated from did not become a site for the armed conflict; it remained on the sidelines of the insurgent activity. But more importantly, he stressed that "they were not touched by the PKK philosophy."

Ayla Akat, a former Peace and Democracy Party (BDP) parliamentarian and spokesperson for the Kurdish Free Women's Congress (Kongreya Jinen Azad, KJA), also highlights the PKK leader Ocalan's approach to gender in addressing and overcoming gender-based inequalities in Kurdish society. The PKK in general and Ocalan in particular, she argues, put women's freedom before national liberation (Akat, Al-Ali, and Tas 2016). This is instructive of wartime experiences interacting with underlying discourses, ideology, and leadership. Absent the ideology and leadership's firm stance toward gender equality, such changes would have been unlikely outcomes of the conflict.

Social-Psychological Linkages

In addition to a progressive ideology and a leadership committed to gender equality, war experiences have also contributed to overcoming social standards of becoming "a good wife and mother." As Caglayan (2010) notes, despite the traumatic impact of conflict, it has also provided opportunities for Kurdish women's activism. In line with those studies that have argued for war dynamics blurring the line between women's private and public roles, the conflict has resulted in an expansion of women's public roles and responsibilities mainly through two mechanisms.

First, while the conflict has generated a surge of internally displaced Kurds, it has also resulted in an increased exposure to forces of modernity. As the Kurdish rural population poured into major cities, female members of displaced families started to get involved more heavily in the Kurdish movement; they became participants in protests, visitors at prisons, and heads of households as caretakers and breadwinners (Celik 2005). Similar to what Menon and Rodgers (2015) found in the case of Nepal, Kurdish women's employment increased as a consequence of the conflict. Some became workers in the garment industry, others seasonal agricultural laborers, while some became self-employed and opened up small shops or became involved with sewing cooperatives.

Local women's councils, organized by the Kurdish movement for recently urbanized Kurdish peasant women, set up sewing cooperatives modeled on those of the Zapatistas in Mexico. One coordinator at these local women's councils underlines the importance of "being involved" with the Kurdish movement in overcoming the challenge of organizing women who were not accustomed to being seen in public, working outside the home, or participating in politics. Being involved with the movement or having ties with it helped the male members of these newly urbanized families to overcome their negative views of women (Tax 2016a, 160).

Intense work at the local level, combined with the conflict and a progressive ideology, has engendered significant changes in Kurdish women's participation in the workforce. Women's increased employment, an element Button (1989, 23) considers to be a sign of social change, has forced many to re-evaluate their beliefs and social norms and has led to the questioning of traditional gender roles.

An analysis of the data on female participation in the labor force in Turkey highlights several important findings. First, overall female participation in the workforce in Turkey is much lower than that of non-Muslim-majority countries with similar levels of economic and political developments. Female employment as a percentage of total labor force in Turkey as of 2015 (31.1 percent) was lower than that of Mexico (32.5 percent), Thailand (45.6 percent), and Romania (46.1 percent) for the year 1996. This shows that even twenty years later, women have a lower participation in the workforce. Second, there is an important gap between the Kurdish east and the rest of Turkey. While the coastal areas and the most industrialized western parts of the country bear a resemblance to Belgium and Italy with women making up more than one-third of the labor force, the eastern regions resemble Algeria and Iran of the late 1990s with ratios around 10 percent.[12]

Nonetheless, Kurdish-majority provinces that became sites of heavy fighting in the 1990s have experienced a significant increase in female participation in the labor force following the forced evacuation of thousands of Kurdish villages. As presented in table 4, data from the Turkish Statistical Institute on female participation in the labor force for the years 2000 and 2004 reinforces this statement.

Of the seven provinces in the eastern and southeastern regions for which the data are available, three are Kurdish majority and are known for their support of the PKK insurgency. The mean percent change for the provinces of Van, Diyarbakir, and Siirt (15.2 percent), which are known for their pro-PKK positions and have been battlefields of the conflict, is nearly twice that of the neighboring provinces of Erzurum, Gaziantep, Malatya, and Kars (8.6 percent), which have yet to show significant support for the PKK and have not become a site of the conflict. While the Kurdish province of Van had a 20 percent increase in its numbers of economically active women between 2000 and 2004, the Turkish-majority province of Erzurum in the same region had a change of 13.6 percent.[13]

In further confirmation of this trend, figure 5 illustrates that Kurdish provinces experienced the highest increase in female participation in the labor force between 2004 and 2011. A report by the Economic Policy Research Foundation of Turkey shows that Kurdish-majority Sanliurfa and Diyarbakir provinces combined experienced a 277.8 percent increase in female participation in the nonagricultural workforce. Another subregion that includes four Kurdish-majority provinces, Mardin, Batman, Sirnak, and Siirt, saw an increase of 275 percent. Female participation in the workforce went up by 225 percent in the subregion including Van, Mus, Bitlis, and Hakkari provinces in the east between 2004 and 2011. Provinces on the margins of the Kurdish region, some of which have Kurdish-majority populations but did not experience the conflict, saw a much lower increase in their female participation rate between 2004 and 2011. Gaziantep, Adiyaman, and Kilis provinces combined saw an increase of 54.3 percent, whereas Agri, Kars, Igdir, and Ardahan collectively saw an increase of 36.4 percent (Asik 2012).

These changes are on a par with the changes in the United States brought about by World War II, described as the most significant event since the Industrial Revolution and one that helped change the social landscape of America (Chafe 1999, x). As Chafe (1999, 11–13) argues, despite the paradoxes and challenges involved (ranging from the lack of a gov-

TABLE 4. Armed Conflict and Women's Employment

Province Name	Conflict Zone	# of Economically Active Women (2000/2004)	% Change
Van	Yes	4,373/5,262	20.33
Diyarbakir	Yes	10,981/12,395	12.88
Siirt	Yes	1,064/1,196	12.41
Erzurum	No	7,645/8,687	13.63
Gaziantep	No	17,200/19,259	11.97
Malatya	No	11,060/12,341	11.58
Kars	No	2,064/2,009	–2.66

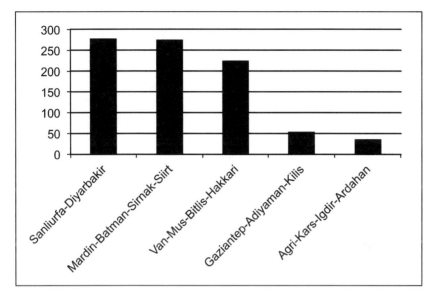

Figure 5. Percentage increase in female participation in labor force, 2004–11

ernmental commitment to gender equality to societal norms and values that confined women to the private sphere), wartime dynamics engendered key changes in the lives of American women. As a result, the female labor force increased by 57 percent. By the time the war came to an end in 1945, women made up 38 percent of all federal workers, more than twice the percentage of the last prewar year.

The second mechanism, in line with the social-psychological linkages outlined in chapter 2, emphasizes the effect of women's participation in war on changing views and attitudes of women. Similar to how the sight of women fighters altered men's perception of women in Uganda (Tripp 2000, 110), a twenty-nine-year-old Yazidi Kurdish man who was trapped on Iraq's Sinjar Mountain by Islamic State fighters before he was saved by a battalion of Kurdish women described the moment as transformative and powerful. He concluded that "the battle made me think of women differently. I'd never thought of women as leaders, as heroes, before" (Wes 2015).

The PKK female units' perseverance has provided a powerful counterimage to that of weak women in need of protection and has played a significant role in redefining gender roles. The very sight of women as fighters serves as a serious challenge to deeply ingrained attitudes regarding traditional gender roles and responsibilities. Many interviewees consistently pointed out female fighters' prowess in explaining their changed views of the opposite gender. One interviewee in his mid-sixties, explaining the shift in his perception of women, stated that "seeing young women fighting for my freedom made me reassess gender issues."[14] Another male interviewee, a thirty-nine-year-old waiter who was detained and tortured for his involvement in the insurgency, noted that war experiences resulted in questioning traditional gender roles and engendered respect for women's strength.

Answers to questions pertaining to gender equality from two subjects confirm the effect of conflict on changing views of women. These two male interviewees were alike in all other characteristics except for that one had little or no exposure to violence. They were born and raised in the same village, lacked formal education, engaged in farming, and were about the same age. When asked about whether men make better political leaders than women, the interviewee with little or no exposure to violence stated that "of course, because women are half-wit." The other interviewee, who was detained for his involvement in the conflict, vehemently opposed that view. Citing women's role in the war against the "state oppression of the Kurds," he stated, "I have known many women who could easily exceed men in several aspects, including leadership skills."

A former female combatant who joined the PKK at an early age and spent more than twenty years with the insurgency maintained that she is a living testament to the transformative aspect of the conflict. This ex-combatant, whom I interviewed for two days in Montreal, Canada, in August 2015, argued that her experiences with the insurgency were life-changing. She asserted that her experiences taught her that a woman can do anything that a man does and that equality between men and women is indeed possible.

A thirty-two-year old male interviewee, whose village was forcibly evacuated by the government in the 1990s, argued that he has grown to be supportive of gender equality and has developed empathy for women as the most marginalized segment of society. In line with the argument made earlier that war dismantles traditional social structures and engenders positive views and attitudes toward women, he concluded that "we [men and women] both suffer equally. Just as the pain does not know gender differences, neither should we." The same interviewee also attributed his changing views and attitudes toward women in part to the urban environment he was thrown into after his family fled. He stated that some progress would have happened absent the conflict but that war dynamics accelerated the change.

Another female interviewee, who was in her fifties and had lost one son in the ranks of the insurgency and saw another imprisoned for his political activism, was transformed into a community organizer. This interviewee, born into a socially conservative society, defied the social norms that confined women to the private sphere and overcame them primarily because of her experiences with the armed conflict. A female medical doctor from Diyarbakir argued that "the conflict has fundamentally changed the patriarchal social culture prevalent in Kurdish society," and a twenty-eight-year-old female accountant stated that the conflict environment has "definitely played a key role in weakening entrenched patriarchal culture among the Kurds."

A closer look at the data collected from these interviews confirms these results. This nonrandom sample of fifty-one interviewees includes a broad range of Kurds such as doctors, lawyers, certified public accountants, school teachers, college students, construction workers, farmers, housewives, and former PKK combatants ranging from twenty-three to sixty-five years of age. The sample included fourteen female and thirty-seven male subjects. A majority of the interviewees had a high school (25 percent) or college degree (45 percent).

The exposure to violence index for this sample ranges from 0.3 to 1 with a mean of 0.69 and a standard deviation of 0.25. Since all subjects were exposed to violence to one degree or another, I compared those individuals with a value of 0.5 or smaller to those with a value greater than 0.5 (n = 23 and 28, respectively). In line with the results obtained from analyzing the probability sample of 2,100 individuals shown below, those with a high level of exposure to violence (>0.5) had significantly more positive attitudes toward women than those with a low level of exposure (< = 0.5). Subjects who experienced a high level of exposure were more likely to disagree with the statements that "Men make better political leaders than women do" and "If a woman earns more money than her husband, it is almost certain to cause problems." Controlling for confounding factors such as age, gender, and education did not substantially change the effect of exposure to violence on disagreeing with the statements regarding women.

War as an Education

Evidence from the Kurdish case also sheds light on the educational aspect of war. Gultan Kisanak describes wartime experiences as "important" in Kurdish women's enlightenment. She explains that as female friends faced state oppression in the form of death, arrests, and torture, they simultaneously began to educate themselves about their rights and defend themselves during trials (Kisanak, Al-Ali, and Tas 2016). In the words of an interviewee, a former mayor who was imprisoned for five years for his alleged support of the PKK, "the Kurds have collectively served a million years in prison." Prison life has hardened many PKK members, sympathizers, or Kurdish civilians caught in conflict dynamics; it has served as a school, if not a university, with many "graduating" as revolutionaries.

Leyla Zana is the Kurdish woman elected to the Turkish National Assembly in 1991. Her parliamentary immunity was lifted so she could be prosecuted for calling for Turkish and Kurdish brotherhood at the oath ceremony, and she was later imprisoned for ten years. Zana was born and raised in a small village in the Kurdish province of Diyarbakir, received no formal education, and was married off in 1975 at age fifteen to a much older cousin, Mehdi Zana, who would later become mayor of Diyarbakir. Her husband's arrest after the military coup of 1980 and her involvement in prison protests led to an arrest in 1988 during which she was tortured and sexually harassed. In her own words, "it was about that time that I began to be a political activist, and when I learned there were Kurdish women fighting with guns I moved to action. . . . This changes everything, I told myself, a woman is also a human being" (Marcus 2007, 173). She became a political activist as a result of her experiences with the conflict.

When asked about the effects of the conflict on women, a thirty-nine-year-old female interviewee (a visual artist who lives in Diyarbakir) stated that "conflict affects the entire society in one form or another, but women often face additional issues and suffer disproportionally. It is much more difficult for women who have lost their husbands, brothers, or sons to cope with the war environment." At the same time, she continued, "as women lived through the conflict they also became politically active and gained confidence, contributing to a more gender-equal society."

It is worthwhile to restate that women's struggle against patriarchal norms and practices in the Kurdish case should not be confused with the prior strength of the women's movement. The Ugandan women's movement consolidated gains in a country with a relatively strong women's movement with roots in pre- and postcolonial mobilization (Tripp 2015), while there was no such women's movement in Kurdish society before the PKK insurgency. In Uganda, girls were already attending secondary schools in the 1920s, which resulted in women working in a variety of professions (Tripp 2015, 55–56). In Turkey, particularly in the Kurdish southeast, female literacy was generally considered at best an unnecessary vice until the early 1980s. Thus women's groups within the Kurdish movement owe their existence largely to war dynamics.

To review, the mechanisms through which conflict dynamics alter gender relations are not independent of one another. They work in conjunction, feeding and influencing each other. To explain the changes the PKK insurrection has engendered, the aforementioned mayor who was removed and later imprisoned for five years on charges of aiding the PKK pointed out two fundamental gains: Kurdishness and gains in women's rights. He argued that Kurdish women have been "reborn" as they are no longer simply "mothers" or "wives." Instead, they are part of public life as fighters, organizers, mayors, and deputies. The PKK leader's views of women and his stance toward gender equality, this interviewee argued, has clearly played a key role in this shift. But, echoing the observation of Gultan Kisanak, the aforementioned comayor of Diyarbakir, that women had to fight for every single advance even within the Kurdish movement, this male interviewee pointed out two additional factors: war dynamics that created opportunities for women, and Kurdish women's own sacrifices for equal treatment within the Kurdish society and movement. Gains in women's rights in the Kurdish case therefore appear to be a result of a combination of war dynamics, a progressive ideology, and a committed leadership.

The rest of this chapter proceeds as follows. First I describe the survey data and lay out the research design to empirically assess the hypothesized effects of exposure to violent conflict on changing views and attitudes toward women. I then proceed to present results from a probability sample of 2,100 individuals from Diyarbakir, Van, and Sanliurfa. The findings show that changes in women's rights are not limited to an increase in women's employment nor are they confined to Kurdish women being elected as mayors or parliamentarians. Instead, war dynamics have engendered positive attitudes toward women in a society that was an unlikely candidate for experiencing such changes.

A Micro-Level Analysis of the War-Women Relationship

As noted above, the pro-Kurdish political parties proportionally have a much higher rate of female representation than any other group of political parties in Turkey. This is due in part to pressure from Kurdish women within the movement and the PKK leader Ocalan's positive approach to gender equality. Is this change a result of the imposition of gender quotas from the top down? To what extent have ordinary Kurds embraced women as mayors, cochairs, and deputies who run committees and oversee municipalities in the Kurdish region? In this section, I present results from an econometric analysis of the key drivers of developing positive attitudes toward women.

To gauge changes in the attitudes toward women, randomly selected participants from three Kurdish-majority provinces in the eastern and southeastern regions of Turkey were asked to express agreement or disagreement with two statements. The first statement aims at measuring the effect of armed conflict on altering perceptions of women as leaders. Participants from Diyarbakir, Van, and Sanliurfa provinces were asked to answer to what extent they agree or disagree with the statement that "Men make better political leaders than women do." The responses are based on values ranging from 1 to 4, where 1 indicates "strongly disagree" and 4 means "strongly agree," with a mean of 2.45 and a standard deviation of 0.69.

Next, respondents were asked to express their opinion of "If a woman earns more money than her husband, it is almost certain to cause problems." Values ranged from "agree" (1), "neither" (2), to "disagree" (3). This variable, which had a mean of 2.33 and a standard deviation of 0.90, is used as a proxy for a different aspect of social change in a society where women are traditionally confined to the private sphere and assigned the roles of good "mothers" or "wives."

I also control for the sociodemographic characteristics of participants. Respondents' ages were measured on a scale of 1–5, where "1" is equal to 18–24, "2" to 25–34, "3" to 35–44, "4" to 45–54, and "5" indicates "55–65." Sex is dichotomized (1 = Female; 0 = Male). More than a third of participants (35 percent) were female. Participants' education level was coded on a scale ranging from 1 to 5, where "1" means "no schooling," "2" indicates "completed primary school," "3" refers to "high school," "4" is "college degree," and "5" indicates a "postgraduate" degree. Nearly 40 percent of respondents had either never attended school or completed only primary education.

Participants' income was measured using the data on whether they owned a car and the number of children they had. Although 53 percent of participants owned a car, more than a third of the sample (37 percent) had four children or more. The Sanliurfa sample had a significantly higher number of children than the other two samples drawn from Diyarbakir and Van.

Religion is often an important aspect of conservative and patriarchal social structures prevalent in many war-torn countries. I utilized the data on "How important is religion in your life?" with responses ranging from 1 to 4, with higher numbers indicating a higher level of religiosity to control for the effect of religiosity on attitudes toward women.

Findings

As demonstrated in table 5, the cumulative measure of exposure to violent conflict is significantly correlated with the two statements used to evaluate attitudes toward women. Model 1 of table 5 presents the findings from an ordered logistic regression on the respondents' agreement with the statement that "men make better political leaders than women," ranging from 1 to 4 with higher numbers indicating agreement with the statement. Thus, the negative coefficient on the exposure to violence index variable indicates less agreement with the statement that male political leaders are superior to female leaders.

Similarly, the coefficient for the exposure to violence variable in model 2 of table 5 corroborates the finding that exposure to violence during the armed conflict results in positive attitudes toward women. The positive

TABLE 5. Exposure to Violence and Attitudes toward Women

Variable	Model 1	% Change	Model 2	% Change
Exposure to Violence Index	−1.08***	−23.3	.35*	9
	[.19]		[.19]	
Sex	−.81***	−32.1	.46***	24.4
	[.09]		[.11]	
Age	−.18***	−16.8	.11**	12.6
	[.05]		[.05]	
Education	−.22	−19	.09	9.2
	[.06]		[.05]	
Automobile	.09	4.9	−.06	−3.3
	[.09]		[.09]	
# of Children	.12***	36.2	−.05**	−5.5
	[.02]		[.02]	
Religiosity	.38***	28.1	−.56***	−31
	[.07]		[.08]	
Cut 1	−2.78		−2.26	
Cut 2	.24		−1.97	
Cut 3	3.18			
N	2100		2100	
Pseudo R^2	.05		.03	
Prob.>Chi^2	<.001		<.001	

Note: * significant at 10 percent;** significant at 5 percent;*** significant at 1 percent level (two-tailed). Robust standard errors in brackets.

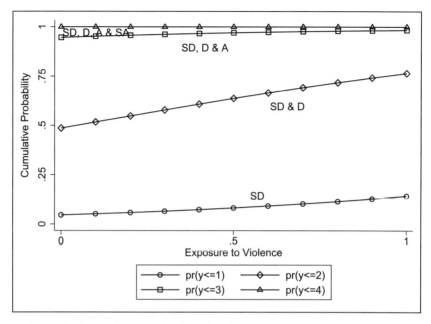

Figure 6. Men are better political leaders than women

coefficient of 0.35 indicates "disagreement" with the statement that "If a woman earns more money than her husband, it is almost certain to cause problems." This provides further evidence for the hypothesized relationship between violence and positive attitudes toward women.[15]

Due to the nonlinear nature of the model, I provide odds ratios to interpret the results obtained using ordered logistic regression. As shown in columns 3 of table 5, one standard deviation increase in the value of exposure to violence index decreases the odds of agreeing with the statement that men make better political leaders than women by 23.3 percent. Furthermore, as illustrated in figure 6, the cumulative probability of "strongly disagree" (SD) and "disagree" (D) with this statement shows a noticeable rise as the exposure to violence index increases. The associated change in the odds for the second statement, "If a woman earns more money than her husband, it is almost certain to cause problems," is 9 percent (column 5 of table 5).

Of the control variables, having more children and being more religious (often deemed characteristics of traditional societies) negatively affect attitudes toward women. The findings on the "sex" variable are not surprising as women are more likely to be supportive of gender equality. The effect of exposure to violence, however, is as robust as that of "sex" and "children."

Contextualizing Violence

The results presented above are consistent with the overall positive relationship between armed conflict and gains in women's rights outlined in current studies. This analysis, however, does not distinguish between different types of exposure to violence, and it fails to account for the effects of ideology on the outcome. As explained in chapter 2, violence during civil war needs to be qualified. In other words, the hypothesized positive effects are likely to be conditioned by three main factors: whether participants experienced violence directly; how they perceive violence and whom they blame for their suffering; and the underlying ideology to which they subscribe.

Different types of exposure to violence might affect the outcome quite differently. Direct exposure in the forms of arrest, torture, or evacuation might condition sufferers differently from indirect forms such as loss of a family member or familiarity with victims of torture or forced eviction. The "direct exposure" variable is set equal to "1" for those individuals who stated that they were arrested, tortured, or fled because of the conflict and "0" otherwise. The mean for this variable was 0.218 with a standard deviation of 0.41. Of the 2,100 respondents, nearly 22 percent were directly exposed, while 78 percent either were not exposed to violence or experienced violence vicariously.[16]

As a part of the framing and blaming processes, participants who blame the rebels for the violence and its negative effects are those who are either complacent about their situations or do not approve of the methods used by the insurgency to seek change. Conversely, individuals who are exposed to violent conflict and blame the state for their victimization are likely to interpret their suffering in such a context that could lead to a positive change in their outlook.

Of the 2,100 individuals 31 percent responded to the question "Who is responsible for these incidents" with "state forces," and 12 percent stated that the rebels/PKK were to be blamed. The rest opted to answer with "others" or "I don't know." While there might be a variety of individual reasons behind the category of "others/I don't know," it is important to stress that the vast majority of violence in the Kurdish case has been a result of confrontations between the PKK and Turkish security forces. In the absence of splinter or rival insurgent groups, violence has been primarily an outcome of the state forces fighting a highly disciplined insurrection. Thus, "others" in this case is likely to be a result of the sensitivity of the question and the conflict environment in which the survey was conducted. As noted above, whether respondents blame the state or rebels is significant because such a response is a stronger indication of how violence is interpreted and framed. Thus the models presented below include "state as perpetrator" and "rebel as perpetrator," using "others" as the reference category.

Finally, while it is difficult to come up with a valid and reliable measure of PKK ideology, respondents' vote choices can serve as a proxy for "support" for the PKK and what it stands for. In line with high levels of political support for the pro-Kurdish political parties and the ruling AKP in the Kurdish region, an overwhelming majority of the respondents stated that they cast their votes for the Kurdish Peace and Democracy Party (BDP) (40 percent) or the AKP (45 percent). The remaining 15 percent stated that they voted for such political parties as the CHP (2.5 percent), the conservative Islamist Felicity Party (Saadet Partisi, 2 percent), the Turkish ultranationalist MHP (2 percent), and the Kurdish Islamist Free Cause Party (HudaPar, 0.5 percent). Five percent of the sample stated that they did not vote.

The main opposition party, the CHP, is known for its prowomen and secular positions. As noted above, though, its vote share in the Kurdish region is negligible. Other parties, such as Saadet, HudaPar, and MHP show similar characteristics with the governing AKP. The Kurdish Islamist HudaPar made an informal coalition with the AKP against the pro-Kurdish HDP in the general elections of November 1, 2015. As Arat (2010, 873) explains at length, the AKP government discourages rather than encourages women's participation in the labor force and propagates patriarchal religious values that endorse traditional gender roles. As a result of this underlying discourse, "religious movements that were once banned establish schools, dormitories and off-campus Quranic courses, socialising the young into religiously sanctioned secondary roles for women" (870).

The practical division of the Kurdish votes between the AKP and the Kurdish BDP offers an opportunity to test for the effects of two different approaches to gender equality. Toward this end, I defined a variable to distinguish the BDP supporters, the Kurdish party at the time the survey was conducted, from others. To be sure, not all BDP voters are hard-core PKK supporters or share its ideology. Nonetheless, they subscribe to what the pro-Kurdish parties advocate, seeking a change in Kurdish-Turkish relations. The underlying ideology often helps set the tone even for those who may not agree with it. Thus voting for the Kurdish party of the time could serve as a reasonable proxy for accounting for the effect of ideology on the outcome.

Table 6 demonstrates results from the models that control for the type of exposure, perpetrator, and ideology as measured above. The negative and significant coefficient on the direct exposure variable indicates that those who were directly exposed to violence in the forms of arrest, torture, or fleeing have more positive attitudes toward women. When compared to

TABLE 6. The Contextual Effect of Violence on Attitudes toward Women

Variable	Model 1	Model 2	Model 3	Model 4
Exposure to Violence Index			-.85***	-.49*
			[.19]	[.28]
Direct Exposure	-.21**	.02		
	[.11]	[.12]		
State as Perpetrator	-.37***	.13		
	[.10]	[.11]		
Rebels as Perpetrator	.19	-.10		
	[.13]	[.14]		
Voted for the BDP	-.35***	.45***	-.38***	-.27***
	[.09]	[.10]	[.09]	[.11]
Exposure* BDP				-.64*
				[.37]
Sex	-.79***	.43***	-.77***	-.77***
	[.09]	[.11]	[.09]	[.09]
Age	-.21***	.14***	-.21***	-.21***
	[.05]	[.05]	[.05]	[.05]
Education	-.20***	.08	-.21***	-.21***
	[.05]	[.05]	[.05]	[.05]
Automobile	.08	-.03	.06	.07
	[.08]	[.09]	[.08]	[.08]
# of Children	.12***	-.06**	.12***	.12***
	[.02]	[.02]	[.02]	[.02]
Religiosity	.33***	-.50***	.33***	.32***
	[.07]	[.08]	[.07]	[.07]
Cut 1	-3.10	-1.84	-3.09	-3.12
Cut 2	-.05	-1.53	-.06	-.08
Cut 3	2.89		2.89	2.86
N	2100	2100	2100	2100
Pseudo R^2	.05	.03	.05	.05
Prob.>Chi^2	<.001	<.001	<.001	<.001

Note: * significant at 10 percent level; ** significant at 5 percent level; significant at 1 percent level (two-tailed). Robust standard errors in brackets.

others, they are less likely to agree with the statement that "men make bet-ter political leaders than women." While 60 percent of self-reported direct victims voiced "disagreement" (7 percent "strongly disagree" and 53 per-cent "disagree") with this statement, only about half (51.6 percent) of oth-ers "disagreed" (6 percent "strongly disagree" and 45 percent "disagree"). Overall, the difference between the subjects who experienced violence directly and others in their attitudes toward gender equality as measured by this statement was statistically discernible [Chi2(3) = 10.42; Pr. = .015].

Similarly, the coefficients on "State as Perpetrator" and "Voted for the BDP" support the argument that the effect of violence is likely to be con-ditioned by how victims interpret it. Compared to "others," those who hold the state responsible for their suffering have more positive attitudes toward women. The direction of the coefficients on "Rebels as Perpetrators" in both models indicates that blaming the rebels is related to lower support for gender equality, but not significantly so. The positive and insignificant coefficient on the variable "Rebels as Perpetrator" in model 1 indicates that those who blame the rebels for the violence are no more or less likely to agree with the statement used to measure support for women as leaders. In addition, in line with the argument made above, the BDP supporters are more likely to see women in a more positive light; they are less likely to agree with the statement that men are better political leaders than women.

The effect of violence on attitudes toward women, measured by responses to the statement "If a woman earns more money than her hus-band, it is almost certain to cause problems," however, is no longer notice-able. As shown in model 2 of table 6, the direct exposure and perpetrator variables do not significantly predict participants' attitudes toward women.

Nonetheless, those who voted for the BDP are significantly more likely to disagree with the statement "If a woman earns more money than her husband, it is almost certain to cause problems." It is important to stress that responses to this statement take values ranging from "agree" to "dis-agree." The average adjusted predictions for BDP voters show that the BDP supporters are less likely than nonsupporters to "agree" with this statement (24 percent as opposed to 33 percent), about as likely to report "neither" (5.7 percent to 6.7 percent), and more likely to "disagree" with this view (70 percent versus 60 percent). The effect of ideology on attitudes toward women as measured by this statement is visualized in figure 7.

To find out if violent conflict impacts the BDP supporters differently than others, I added an interaction term between the "Exposure to Violence Index" and "Voted for the BDP" variables. In model 3 of table 6, I account for the ideology of the PKK while keeping all other variables the same as in

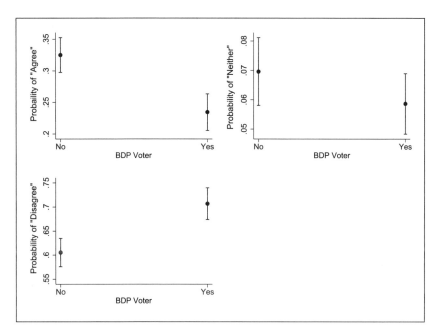

Figure 7. If a woman earns more money than her husband, it is almost certain to cause problems

model 1 of table 5. Model 4 of table 6 includes an interactive term between "Exposure to Violence Index" and "Voted for the BDP" variables.

In model 3, measures of exposure to violence and ideology are both highly significant in the expected direction; they are negatively and significantly related to the statement that men make better political leaders than women. In model 4, where these two variables interact, the effect of the exposure index is reduced both substantively and statistically. The interaction term is negative, albeit the coefficient on this variable (as with the exposure index) is marginally significant.

Alternative model specifications also showed that while the effect of exposure to violence on having positive attitudes toward women is apparent, this effect is not as robust as argued in current studies. The results also suggest that the hypothesized effect of violence is likely to be more complicated than is portrayed in the existing literature.[17] Significantly, such an effect is in part a result of violence interacting with other variables. In line with the argument made in chapter 2 and consistent with insights from the qualitative data, results from these models strengthen the overall conclusion that the effect of violent conflict on gains in women's rights is conditioned by the framing of violence. Moreover, the underlying discourse constitutes an important part. In addition, changes in women's rights are multifaceted. Violence might assist overcoming one aspect of gender-based discrimination but fail to address another.

A closer look at the data collected from the in-depth interviews confirms these findings. While exposure to violence has facilitated paving the way for more gender-equal positions toward women, its effect is not straightforward. Those interviewees who were well-versed in the PKK's underlying ideology were more articulate about their changing attitudes toward women. They could make sense of the changes that Kurdish society has been undergoing and relate to these changes at a level that is likely to leave a lasting legacy. Those who were "involved" with the Kurdish movement displayed similar yet less elaborate views. While they were less successful in articulating the changes they or society were experiencing, the effect of the PKK's positive stance toward women was visible. The PKK's discourse on women has provided a vernacular with which many Kurds make sense of an otherwise chaotic and devastating armed conflict.[18]

Conclusion

This chapter demonstrates that although the effect of armed conflict on changing attitudes toward women is not as straightforward as depicted in the existing studies, it is noticeable. Evidence from the Kurdish case shows that war dynamics impact gender relations and help break traditional roles assigned to women. Gains in women's rights are observable in economic, social, military, and political spheres. Women are progressively becoming visible in public life. They are increasingly participating in the workforce, serving as mayors and cochairs, running committees, supervising local councils, and engaging in the armed struggle as fighters.

The roles war dynamics play in producing these positive changes is conditioned mainly by the insurgent ideology and a committed leadership. Without the leadership, direction, and vision provided by the PKK leader Ocalan, the positive changes in gender relations described in this chapter might not have been realized. In light of evidence from in-depth interviews and a large probability survey, this chapter shows that the mechanisms through which improvements in women's rights occur are not necessarily isolated from one another. Violent conflict transforms mainly through interacting with the underlying insurgent ideology.

Clearly, the survey data measures one aspect of gender equality, and it is hard to infer a change in behavior from the data at hand. Hours-long interviews, however, with dozens of individuals (some of which were conducted at interviewees' homes) revealed that the change described here is more than just a simple "disagree" answer to a survey question. Many male interviewees, especially those who lost a family member or witnessed violence personally, demonstrated significantly more positive behavior toward their wives, daughters, or sisters. Female members of families who had "sacrificed," a term that denotes families with a son or daughter in the PKK, showed important differences than female members of families with otherwise similar characteristics. Women in the first group were more vocal in expressing their hopes, ambitions, and frustrations. They also enjoyed freedom of mobility and greater freedom in their choice of dress.

While these issues might be taken for granted in the Western context, traditional societies are often characterized by their restrictions on women's mobility and dress. This is particularly so for Muslim-majority societies. Norris and Inglehart (2004; also see Inglehart and Norris 2003), in their extensive analysis of cultural values from the World Values Survey, conclude that while there are no significant differences between the populations in the West and the Muslim world in their approval of democracy, they differ significantly in their support for equal rights and opportunities for women.

Women's mobility and dress became one of the first issues in the aftermath of the revolutionary waves collectively referred to as the Arab Spring, which swept through the Arab world in late 2010 and early 2011. Women, especially those unaccompanied by a male relative, were accused of immorality and assaulted for wearing short skirts (Gurses 2015c). Turkey's deputy prime minister Bulent Arinc, a founding member of the AKP, called for chastity in both men and women in 2014 and urged women not to laugh in public (Dearden 2014). Thus, the freedom to appear in public without a headscarf, wearing pants, or without a male relative signifies an important change in gender relations.

To be sure, gender equality or women's empowerment is not confined to the changes described in this study. Furthermore, as in the case of Rwanda, Kurdish women still suffer from patriarchal control. Similar to what Uvuza (2014, 199) argues with regard to the limitations of conflict-gender equality relationships in Rwanda (i.e., biases, stereotypes, and discrimination still exist both in the home and workplace), Kurdish women continue to suffer from the entrenched patriarchal norms and values.

While conflict might fail to eradicate traditional patriarchal values that often determine the role and status of women in social hierarchy, it clearly weakens the prewar patriarchy, leads to wartime partnership, and results in at least "partial post-war empowerment" (Blumberg 2001, 163). Furthermore, as Thames and Williams (2015, 3) have demonstrated, "women's representation in one area or institution does, in fact, affect women's representation in other areas." This process of "contagion," the authors conclude, manifests itself in different ways and especially in the area of political representation, where "even small gains . . . can have significant effects down the road" (127–28).

In the span of three decades, Kurdish society has certainly shaken off its socially conservative culture and embraced a remarkable shift toward gender equality. This transformation in gender roles and relations is substantial and, as Bengio (2016, 45–46) notes, is "deep and authentic" enough "to not allow for the return to earlier repressive norms and traditional roles." The conflict has been a primary engine of social change. It has created new contexts and possibilities for the most marginalized segment of society, and the insurgent ideology together with a committed leadership has both facilitated and solidified these new possibilities.

## FOUR

War and Political Culture

Citizenship rights as entitlements are subject to bargaining between states and specific groups of subjects trying to redefine their relations with the polity. While these mutually recognizable rights may be negotiable, they are historically a primary outcome of resistance and struggle (Tilly 1998). Reflective of this line of argument, an increasingly growing literature has pointed to the democratizing potential of civil war. Civil conflict, these studies argue, can create opportunities for balanced power relations, redistribute economic and political powers among the contending forces, and facilitate democratization after the war. Civil war may lead to more inclusive polities, especially when bargains over power sharing are formalized in a negotiated settlement (Wood 2000, 2001; Wantchekon 2004; Gurses and Mason 2008; Joshi 2010; Nilsson 2012; Armey and McNab 2015).

In this chapter, I argue that civil war not only sparks the seed of change by radically reshaping social relations at the macro level but can also engender changes in the political culture at the micro level. Focusing on the Kurdish insurgency in Turkey, I explore how wartime experiences (1) engender norms and attitudes that are favorable to democracy at the individual level, (2) create politically active participants with a sense of empowerment, (3) contribute to the nation-building process by forging a shared identity with which members of warring groups identify.

As presented below, results from a large probability sample of 2,100 individuals indicate that exposure to violent conflict is associated with greater support for political activism. Concurrently, wartime experiences account for politically active participants with a sense of empowerment.

Evidence from systematic in-depth interviews sheds additional light on this asserted causal relationship.

Consistent with the social-psychological mechanism outlined in chapter 2, wartime experiences have induced a sense of dignity and resilience. Assertiveness demonstrated by taking their fate in their own hands appears to be one of the features that characterize Kurds involved with the movement or who suffered because of it. Moreover, the armed conflict has contributed to a sense of belonging and a shared identity among Kurds exposed to the war.

War and Individual Empowerment

Civil wars are often products of sociopolitical environments characterized by resentment, discontent, and repression. Violence, as a defining feature of civil war, occurs when our sense of justice is offended (Arendt 1969). As the conflict disrupts and dismantles the socioeconomic fabric of the society, experiences during civil war can potentially engender "a progressive practice of empowerment and pluralization" (Tønder 2013, 11–12). This creates a situation in which victims recounting their own suffering not only develop empathy but also show a strong will and desire to grow beyond themselves. Seeing history as a possibility, something that can be transformed, sufferers no longer see themselves as objects but instead as responsible subjects (Freire 2000, 36). One potential outcome of this ongoing engagement and experimentation is what one scholar of democracy calls *"the logic of equality"* from which democratic participation develops (Dahl 1998, 10, italics in original).

As wartime experiences lead to a greater awareness of real or perceived injustices within the system, this "logic of equality" is bound to push for a process of democratic contestation characterized by greater engagement and participation. This "voluntary and individual participation" as opposed to "passive obedience and social deference," Crick (2002, 94) notes, makes up a key aspect of modern democracy. Despite the harm inflicted during the war, wartime dynamics could lead to the rise of a democratic character defined by a responsibility to create a community "in which human dignity is realized in theory and practice" (Lasswell 1951, 473).

Thus the war, with its shocks and traumas, has the capacity to restore and construct just as it destroys. It may facilitate a change from which a dissident culture arises. This effect is borne out by results from a series of regression models presented below. An analysis of the survey data along with the insights from interviews lend support for the argument that violence during civil war is positively linked to greater political activism.

An Empirical Analysis of Violence and Political Activism

To assess the effect of civil war on political activism, respondents were asked to express their approval or disapproval of a list of actions that people take to achieve political goals. These actions include legal political activism (e.g., participating in legal demonstration or working on an electoral campaign for a political party or candidate) as well as support for violent change (e.g., supporting violence to pursue political goals and closing or blocking roads).

As demonstrated in table 7, the responses were based on values ranging from 1 to 7, where 1 means "strongly disapprove" and 7 indicates "strongly approve." I constructed a summary measure of support for political activism by taking the average of the support for the actions listed in table 7. To make interpretation easier, I then rescaled the resulting variable to take values between 0 and 1, so that 0 represents very low support for political activism and 1 represents very high support for political activism. This summary measure of activism ranges from 0.12 to 1 with a mean of 0.52.

To explore the relationship between exposure to violence during the civil war and political activism, I conducted an ordinary least squares (OLS) regression analysis. The regression results indicate a strong positive relationship between these two variables even after controlling for the effect

TABLE 7. Measuring Support for Political Activism

Variable	Min	Max	Mean	Std. Deviation
People participate in legal demonstrations	1	7	5.72	1.81
People work on electoral campaign for a political party or candidate	1	7	5.99	1.50
People participate in the closing or blocking of roads	1	7	2.52	2.01
People take the law into their own hands when the state does not punish criminals	1	7	2.74	2.20
Using violence to pursue political goals is justified	1	7	1.57	1.35
Political Activism Index	.12	1	.52	.15

of several socioeconomic variables. As presented in table 8, the coefficients on the exposure index, the central explanatory variable defined earlier, is consistent with earlier studies that have pointed out positive political outcomes of civil war (Wood 2003; Bellows and Miguel 2009; Blattman 2009; Voors et al. 2012). The findings indicate that individuals who were exposed to violence during the civil conflict seem to have a higher degree of support for political activism.

The statistical findings from model 1 are visualized in figure 8. As shown, violence is positively associated with an increasing support for political activism. Of the control variables, female respondents show a greater support for political activism; to the contrary, self-identified religious individuals, those with higher levels of income as measured by owning a car, and older respondents show less support for the list of activities used to gauge support for political activism.[1]

To distinguish between potential qualitative differences between support for participating in a legal demonstration, working on an electoral campaign for a political party or candidate, and approval of violence to

TABLE 8. OLS Regression Results for Violence and Support for Political Activism

Variable	Model 1	Model 2 [Non-violent]	Model 3 [Violent]	Model 4 [Diyarbakir]	Model 5 [Van]	Model 6 [Sanliurfa]
Exposure to Violence Index	.14*** [.01]	.16*** [.01]	.14*** [.01]	.13*** [.01]	.17*** [.02]	.19*** [.003]
Sex	.08*** [.007]	−.005 [.01]	.13*** [.01]	.05*** [.01]	.10*** [.01]	.07*** [.01]
Age	−.01*** [.004]	.006 [.006]	−.03*** [.005]	−.01** [.006]	−.01* [.007]	−.01 [.007]
Education	.005 [.004]	.04*** [.006]	−.02*** [.005]	.004 [.007]	.01* [.007]	.001 [.006]
Automobile	−.01*** [.006]	−.004 [.009]	−.02*** [.008]	−.03*** [.01]	−.01 [.01]	.002 [.01]
# of Children	.009 [.001]	−.002 [.002]	.01*** [.002]	.005* [.003]	.01*** [.003]	.004 [.003]
Religiosity	−.03*** [.005]	−.03*** [.007]	−.04*** [.007]	−.02*** [.007]	−.02** [.01]	−.04*** [.008]
Constant	.59*** [.02]	.75*** [.04]	.47*** [.03]	.59*** [.04]	.53*** [.05]	.64 [.04]
N	2100	2100	2100	7000	700	700
R^2	.16	.11	.21	.17	.19	.16
Prob.>F	<.0001	<.0001	<.0001	<.0001	<.0001	<.0001

Note: * significant at 10 percent level; *** significant at 1 percent level (two-tailed). Robust standard errors in brackets.

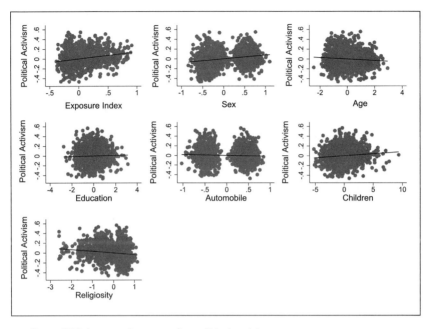

Figure 8. Violence and support for political activism

pursue political goals, I analyzed the data by breaking down the political activism index into nonviolent and violent political activism indices. Such analysis, as shown in models 2 and 3 of table 8, produced substantially the same results. Exposure to violence positively and significantly predicts support for political activism regardless of how it is constructed.

There are, however, some noticeable changes in the effect of the education, age, and sex variables on the support for violent versus nonviolent political activism. Consistent with rational choice explanations that have pointed out the effect of education and income on risk aversion (Mason and Murtagh 1985; Humphreys and Weinstein 2008), respondents with higher levels of education are supportive of nonviolent political activism whereas they significantly disapprove of engaging in violence to pursue political goals. Similarly, those who own an automobile, as a measure of high income, and older respondents oppose violent political activism.

Female respondents and those with more children are supportive of the use of violence (such as closing or blocking of roads) to pursue political goals. One likely explanation for this finding is that many women in Kurdish society tend to perceive the insurgent movement as an escape from the patriarchal social structure that has subjugated them and makes them dependent on men. Thus the PKK's strategic use of violence accompanied with its antitraditional stance explains support for the use of violence as a facilitator of change among the poor and women, the two most disfranchised subgroups of Kurdish society.

As an additional robustness test, I analyzed the data for each province separately to account for potential qualitative differences between the three provinces. As shown in models 4–6 of table 8, the hypothesized effect of exposure to violence holds across all models. With some minor changes in the direction and sign of some of the control variables, the findings from these separate models confirm the positive link between exposure to violence and support for political activism.

To account for the argument that violence alone might fail to produce changes in political culture (i.e., violence needs to be examined within a context), I added variables that control for perpetrator, type of exposure to violence, and respondents' vote choice as a proxy for ideology. The inclusion of variables that control for perpetrator and ideology to the basic model (model 1 of table 8) indicates that although respondents who hold the state responsible and those who voted for the Kurdish party are significantly more likely to lend greater support for political activism, violence seems to have an independent effect on producing support for activism.

As shown in model 1 of table 9, the "State as Perpetrator" and "Voted for the BDP" variables have noticeable positive effects on the outcome. The results from an alternative model specification, which includes an interaction term between exposure to violence and voting for the Kurdish BDP (model 2), yields substantively the same results. While this model fails to produce a significant effect for the interaction term, it nonetheless confirms the significant positive effect violence has on the outcome.

Furthermore, these findings, in line with the argument made in the theory chapter, point to the importance of a framing process. As evidenced by the insignificant coefficient on the "Rebels as Perpetrator" variable, respondents who blame the rebels for their suffering have not experienced a change in their political culture as defined above.

Model 3 controls for the type of exposure. Consistent with the findings obtained in the previous chapter, respondents who have experienced violence directly have a higher level of support for political activism than those who experienced violence indirectly.

Insights from in-depth interviews vindicate these findings. One interviewee, who was detained and tortured for aiding the PKK, complained of sleep disturbances and nightmares tied to his experiences under arrest.

This interviewee, who now resides in Toronto, Canada, pointed out that his experiences have imbued him with a sense of righteousness. "Anytime I see unfair treatment, I feel the urge to fight injustice." This sentiment is in line with the argument that wartime experiences can help develop and strengthen righteous impulses.

Further, exposure to violence has also generated a sense of empowerment and agency. Echoing Kisanak's conclusion that "my life in prison" helped me "destroy fear" and "develop self-confidence" (Kisanak, Al-Ali, and Tas 2016), this interviewee noted that "as I began to participate in the movement I overcame the fear. I learned how to live with it. The fear of the police or repression ceased to be an obstacle in the way of

TABLE 9. Accounting for the Context: Violence and Support for Political Activism

Variable	Model 1	Model 2	Model 3
Exposure to Violence Index	.07***	.09***	
	[.01]	[.01]	
Direct Exposure			.02***
			[.008]
State as Perpetrator	.04***	.04***	.05***
	[.007]	[.0 07]	[.007]
Rebels as Perpetrator	−.01	−.01	−.008
	[.009]	[.009]	[.009]
Voted for the BDP	.05***	.06***	.06***
	[.007]	[.008]	[.006]
Exposure* BDP		−.03	
		[.02]	
Sex	.07***	.07***	.07***
	[.007]	[.007]	[.007]
Age	−.01***	−.01***	−.01***
	[.004]	[.004]	[.004]
Education	.003	.003	.003
	[.004]	[.004]	[.004]
Automobile	−.01**	−.01**	−.01**
	[.006]	[.006]	[.006]
# of Children	.007***	.007***	.008***
	[.001]	[.001]	[.001]
Religiosity	−.02***	−.02***	−.02***
	[.005]	[.005]	[.005]
Constant	.53***	.53***	.54***
	[.02]	[.02]	[.002]
N	2100	2100	2100
R^2	.20	.21	.20
Prob.>F	<.0001	<.0001	<.0001

Note: ** significant at 5 percent level; *** significant at 1 percent level (two-tailed). Robust standard errors in brackets.

contributing to what I believed in." Similarly, when asked about how he would describe the most important impact of his experiences during his eleven years in the ranks of the PKK, a former PKK combatant stated "my experiences as a guerrilla taught me that there is always a way, that I can bring about change."

Experiences of another interviewee are noteworthy and help shed further light on the link between exposure to violence and change in political culture. This interviewee was in his mid-fifties, had no formal education, and was forced to evacuate his village in the 1990s. He was arrested and tortured by state authorities numerous times and lost a son serving in the ranks of the PKK. Akin to what Fanon (2004, 2) calls "decolonization," a process by which a new man is created, he spoke of his experiences as emancipatory or liberating despite tragic losses and suffering endured during the very same involvement. Consistent with the argument that exposure to civil war is likely to result in greater awareness of self, he asserted that "I have gotten to know myself because of my experiences with the insurgency. I feel like I am a better, enlightened person now."

Similarly, experiences of a forty-one-year old male ex-combatant, who now resides in Belgium as an asylum seeker, offer another example of the transformative nature of the war. This interviewee joined the insurrection at the age of nineteen, shortly after graduating high school. He fought in the ranks of the PKK for four years before he was captured and incarcerated for ten years. As a teenager in the 1990s, he experienced political discrimination and humiliation. This former militant highlighted injustices within the system in his decision to join the insurgents. Echoing a response given by a twenty-year-old Colombian regarding why he joined the FARC—"I got angry, so I joined the FARC to fight back" (Brodzinsky 2016)—this interviewee stated that "it was injustices and unequal treatment of me and people around me that made me reconsider who I was and resulted in joining the rebels in the mountains."

One event, he noted, left a lasting print on him: "One day on my way back to home from high school, I saw the body of a PKK guerrilla laying in the back of a dirty trailer sitting in front of the police station. That moment embodied the injustices that we suffered. My dignity as a human being took a hit. Even our dead bodies are not respected, I said to myself. The PKK movement provided an option, perhaps the only venue, to express my anger, to do something about the situation." He left for the mountains soon after.

Consistent with Arendt's (1969) interpretation that violence occurs when our sense of justice is offended, the desire for equality, freedom, and dignity outplayed his family's plans of him becoming a doctor or an engineer. This ex-PKK militant whom I interviewed for ten days in Belgium in June 2015, reflecting on his experiences in the mountains and prison, concluded after a moment of silent deliberation, "I believe my participation in the rebellion overall has been a positive experience. I have gained a broader perspective on life."

When asked what changed her opinion of the Kurdish minority's treatment in the country, a sixty-five-year-old woman with no formal education wholeheartedly stated, "I could not justify it any longer." Another male interviewee in his late sixties, who was repeatedly arrested in the 1990s for refusing to join the "village guards" against the insurgency, answered the question, "Why didn't you just do what many others did, join the village guards to avoid state punishment and receive material benefits?" with "my dignity would not let me."

Some of these interviewees, who were quite oblivious to their political environment until they were drawn into the conflict-charged environment, engaged and developed a consciousness as a result of their experiences with the armed conflict. It evoked a sense of justice from which a sense of responsibility arose. The war situation resulted in breaking the barrier of fear, defending their dignity, bringing up hidden strengths, and inducing talent and energy that many of the participants did not know they possessed.

It should be noted that the PKK's violent engagement with the Turkish state illustrates only one aspect of its struggle. The PKK has long portrayed itself as a revolutionary movement of freedom (Ozgurluk Hareketi) and emphasized political education to raise political awareness among its supporters. Its leader Ocalan makes frequent references to "free life" (*ozgur yasam*) in outlining the PKK's ideology and key goal of creating new identities. While the PKK does not provide formal education, due primarily to its lack of control of territory, it sets up academies and schools in its training camps outside Turkey with an emphasis on critical self-awareness. This "PKK education," Westrheim (2014, 140, 151) argues, is partly responsible for "moving away from a state of collective amnesia to a collective critical awareness."

Nonetheless, while the statistical models show that voting for the Kurdish political party has a detectable effect on support for political activism, the inclusion of the measures of ideology does not produce any meaningful changes to the strong positive effect the exposure index has on the outcome, as shown in models 1 and 2. Furthermore, in contrast to the frequent references made to PKK ideology as a key factor behind changes in women's rights noted in the previous chapter, none of the interviewees ascribed the changes they experienced to the insurgent group's ideology. Instead, wartime dynamics appear to have invoked a sense of justice, as evidenced by interviewees citing "conscience" and "dignity" to explain the changes they experienced. Thus, although the insurgent group's ideology might have facilitated the rise of a dissident culture in a way that the statistical models might fail to capture, wartime experiences (particularly the sociopsychological mechanism and educational aspect of war dynamics) seem to better explain the rise of assertive individuals, which constitutes an important aspect of change in political culture.

Taken together, these findings suggest that the effect of violence on the political culture of participants appears to be more noticeable and direct than the effect violence has on changing views and attitudes toward women. Clearly, this might be a result of measurements or data used to delineate the complex relationship between war and change. The findings also indicate that a shift in social culture as discussed in the previous chapter might be far more complicated and challenging than a change in political culture.

War and Support for Democracy

Before I turn to the war–nation-building nexus, it is worth addressing another aspect of political culture. As noted above, a number of studies have pointed to the democratizing potential of war. Markedly, countries in which costly civil wars were brought to an end with a negotiated agreement experienced a noticeable democratization in the postwar era. How do wartime experiences influence participants' views and attitudes toward democracy at the micro level? Do individuals become more supportive of democracy as a result of war?

I begin by presenting results from the survey data on the link between wartime experiences and support for democracy, and then highlight the context to qualify the purported positive link between these two variables. Support for democracy is measured by the responses to the question, "Democracy may have problems, but it is better than any other form of government. To what extent do you agree?," which takes values ranging from 1 to 7, where 1 means "not at all" and 7 indicates "a lot." This variable had a mean of 5.6 with a standard deviation of 1.7. Results from the models that statistically assess the effect of violence on the level of support for different institutions and democracy are presented in table 10.

As shown in models 1 and 2, the effect of the exposure index on support for democracy is not as robust as the effect violence has on support for political activism. An ordered logistic regression yields a positive and significant coefficient, indicating that individuals with higher levels of exposure to violence show greater support for democracy (model 1). This effect, however, is sensitive to the choice of statistical method. Model 2 demonstrates that the use of an OLS regression renders this relationship insignificant. Moreover, the BDP voters appear to have a significantly lower level of support for democracy, as demonstrated in models 1 and 2.

At first glance, this finding runs counter to studies that have found sup-

TABLE 10. Violence and Support for Democracy

Variable	Model 1 (Ordered Logit)	Model 2 (OLS)	Model 3 (OLS)	Model 4 (OLS)	Model 5 (Logit)
Exposure to Violence	.75***	.26	−1.20***	−1.18***	.98***
Index	[.22]	[.19]	[.19]	[.18]	[.21]
State as Perpetrator	.03	−.04	−.60***	−.73***	.26**
	[.11]	[.10]	[.10]	[.10]	[.11]
Rebels as	.39***	.32***	.36***	.30**	−.25*
Perpetrator	[.12]	[.10]	[.11]	[.14]	[.15]
Voted for the BDP	−.47***	−.41***	−1.86***	−1.28***	.46***
	[.09]	[.08]	[.09]	[.09]	[.10]
Sex	.18***	−.10	−.31***	.32***	−.39***
	[.05]	[.08]	[.08]	[.09]	[.10]
Age	−.21***	.17**	.01	−.02	.09
	[.05]	[.05]	[.05]	[.05]	[.05]
Education	.19***	.11	−.16***	−.36***	.08
	[.05]	[.05]	[.05]	[.05]	[.05]
Automobile	.10	.11	−.03	.03	−.17**
	[.08]	[.07]	[.08]	[.08]	[.09]
# of Children	−.04*	−.03	.04**	.03	−.08***
	[.02]	[.06]	[.02]	[.02]	[.02]
Religiosity	.05	−.005	.44***	.18***	−.04
	[.06]	[.06]	[.06]	[.06]	[.07]
Constant		4.96***	4.45***	4.91***	−.53
		[.31]	[.35]	[.36]	[.40]
Cut 1	−1.75				
Cut 2	−1.44				
Cut 3	−.99				
Cut 4	−.13				
Cut 5	.58				
Cut 6	1.26				
N	2100	2100	2100	2100	2100
(Pseudo) R^2	.018	.038	.37	.27	.059
Prob.>Chi²/F	<.0001	<.0001	<.0001	<.0001	<.0001

Note: * significant at 10 percent level; ** significant at 5 percent level; significant at 1 percent level (two-tailed). Robust standard errors in brackets.

porters of pro-Kurdish political parties more supportive of concessions (Kibris 2011) and that Kurds in Turkey are significantly less likely than Turks to support authoritarianism (Belge and Karakoc 2015). How can these seemingly unexpected findings be explained? A closer analysis of the data below clarifies that these findings do not necessarily demonstrate a lower support for democracy among those who are subjected to violence or among supporters of the Kurdish political party. Instead, the results vindicate the importance of the context with which sufferers make sense of their sacrifices or losses.

As the findings on the perpetrator variables indicate, those who blame the rebels for their suffering lend greater support for democracy (models 1 and 2) and show higher levels of trust in the national government (model 3). Trust in the national government is measured on a similar scale used to assess support for democracy. In other words, participants were asked to state their level of trust in the national government on a scale ranging from 1 ("not at all") to 7 ("a lot").

Using responses to "trust in the justice system," which was measured on the same scale, yielded basically the same findings as shown in model 4. Thus, individuals who blame the violence and its consequences on the PKK show significantly higher levels of trust in the national government and judicial system. Whereas those who accuse the state of being the culprit for the violent situation have a significantly lower levels of trust in the national government (model 3) and the legal system (model 4).

Results from a model that gauges the effect of violence on support for local governance corroborate the contextual aspects of wartime violence as well as democracy. Respondents were asked about whether they think the municipality should be given more powers and responsibilities. The answers included (a) More for the municipality, (b) National government should assume greater responsibility, (c) Nothing should change, (d) More to the municipality if it provides better services, and (e) Doesn't know/Doesn't respond.

These responses should be qualified and scrutinized within the Turkish context. While governorship positions in Turkey carry significant powers, governors are not elected by a popular vote. They are appointed by the government. Furthermore, the 10 percent electoral threshold introduced after the 1980s, which prevents any political party from gaining seats in the national parliament unless they receive at least 10 percent of the total votes cast, has essentially blocked Kurdish political parties from national representation.

The Kurdish HDP became the first Kurdish political party to overcome this electoral obstacle in the June 7, 2015 general elections. This outcome contributed to ending the AKP dominance in parliament by precluding it from forming a majority government. It did not, however, lead to any meaningful changes in Kurdish access to state power. The aftermath of the June elections marked the end of the two-year-old fragile ceasefire between the Turkish government and the PKK. Critics charge that the Erdogan-controlled government deliberately resorted to violence to stoke nationalist sentiments and regain control of the legislature.

The Kurdish HDP's election bureaus, rallies, and officials were violently targeted, resulting in scores of casualties. The National Intelligence Organization (Milli Istihbarat Teskilati, MIT) allegedly held secret meetings with heads of influential tribes in several Kurdish provinces, notably in Sanliurfa and Bingol where the HDP made significant gains in the June elections, to coerce or cajole them into voting for the AKP. The Free Cause Party (HudaPar) of Kurdish Islamists announced it would not participate in the next elections. While the HudaPar's vote share is negligible nationwide, it helped the AKP win additional seats in the Kurdish region.[2]

The follow-up snap elections of November 1, 2015 were held in an increasingly authoritarian environment and resulted in the HDP losing a significant number of seats it had previously won in the Turkish National Assembly, down from eighty to fifty-nine, after barely surpassing the 10 percent threshold. The HDP continued to come under severe pressure after the November elections. In May 2016 it was accused of being the PKK's political wing, and some of its members of Parliament were stripped of their parliamentary immunity from prosecution. In November 2016 the HDP's coleaders, Selahattin Demirtas and Figen Yuksekdag, along with nine other HDP parliamentarians were arrested on charges of "terrorist propaganda."

Although the survey was conducted shortly before the collapse of the ceasefire and the repressive measures described above, Kurdish underrepresentation within the political system is not limited to tumultuous times. One recent study documents extensively that in clear contrast to the official rhetoric of equal access for all, Kurds in Turkey have historically faced a high level of discrimination in accessing state power. They are ominously underrepresented in the upper echelons of state bureaucracy including the military, governorship positions, ministerial appointments, and high judiciary. This pattern of underrepresentation not only precedes the onset of the PKK insurgency but is also resistant to changes in regime or government since the formation of modern Turkey in 1923. The transition to multiparty democracy in the 1950s and the rise of Islamists (who had long blamed the secular center-right or center-left parties for the Kurdish issue and espoused a platform of Islamic unity, which they argued transcends ethnic identities) to power in the 2000s has failed to redress the Kurdish exclusion from the state (Tezcur and Gurses 2017).

This situation leaves municipality-level governance as essentially the only noteworthy elected position through which Kurds could exercise their right to meaningfully participate in the democratic process. The sister party of the HDP, the Peace and Democracy Party (BDP), campaigned in the March 2014 local elections with the slogan "freedom through self-governance" and swept the polls in the Kurdish regions, winning mayoral elections in 103 municipalities including such major cities as Diyarbakir, Van, and Mardin.[3]

Given the context, support for mayoral powers and responsibilities could serve as a more valid measure to evaluate Kurdish support for democracy. I recoded the responses to the question pertaining to municipality-level responsibility into two categories to better assess the link between violence and support for greater decentralization or devaluation of power to the local level. Those who stated that municipalities should be granted more powers were coded "1," and all others were assigned a score of "0."

As presented in model 5, the three variables that significantly predict the outcome of "greater powers and responsibilities to municipality-level governance" are those that were found to be robust predictors of support for political activism and positive attitudes toward women. That is, a high level of exposure to violence and being a BDP supporter positively and significantly affect support for more rights and responsibilities to municipal authority. Converting the logit estimates into predicted probabilities shows that being a BDP voter increases the predicted probability of support for granting more powers and responsibilities to local level governance by 0.12. As demonstrated in figure 9, a change in the value of exposure to violence index from no exposure ("0") to maximum exposure ("1"), while holding other variables at their means, increases the same probability by 0.24.

In further confirmation of the results on the perpetrator variables in models 1 through 4, the outcome is greatly shaped by whom individuals blame for their suffering. The positive and significant coefficient on the "State as Perpetrator" variable indicates that those who blame the state are more likely to support granting more rights to local government, whereas those who hold the rebels responsible for the violence oppose such devolution of power, as evidenced by the negative coefficient on this variable.

Taken together, the results suggest a nuanced conclusion. The analysis

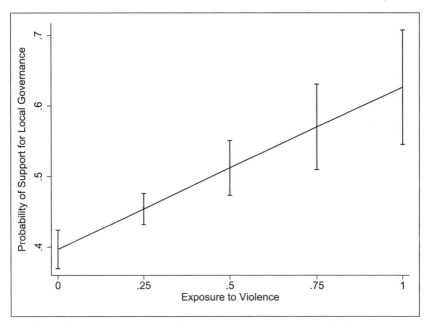

Figure 9. Violence and support for decentralization among the Kurds

reveals that support for democracy is conditioned primarily by one's definition of democracy and her position in the system. As in the case of Kurds in Turkey, when democracy is confined to holding elections, or when the system by and large disfranchises a subset of the population, or when the democratic system in place relegates that group into the permanent position of an outsider, support for such a form of government will surely be low among members of such a group.

Not surprisingly, and as a reflection of overall Kurdish dissatisfaction with the political system and quest for justice, when asked "in a few words, what does democracy mean for you?" nearly half of the sample, 44 percent, answered "freedom." While "equality" (13 percent) and "justice" (7 percent) were the other two most common expressions used to define what democracy should entail. Thus, the findings cumulatively indicate a growing sense of alienation and dissatisfaction from the way "democracy" is practiced rather than Kurdish lack of support for it. In this context, little or no support for "democracy" along with strong support for local-level governance represents a challenge to the practice and conceptualization of democracy by the majority and confirms the thesis advanced earlier that wartime experiences are associated with the emergence of a participant political culture at the micro level.

War and Nation Building

The armed conflict examined here falls within the ethnic civil war category, which often includes secessionist or ethnonationalist insurgencies. Such civil wars involve groups that are at odds with the identity of a state and hence fight to reconfigure ethnic relations. As noted in chapter 3, despite the PKK's efforts to avoid lapsing into a narrow form of nationalism, as an autonomy-seeking movement and an insurgency that almost exclusively recruits from ethnic Kurds in Turkey and beyond, it can be classified as an ethnonationalist insurgency.

As explained in the theory chapter, ethnonationalist rebel groups, as the rival claimants to power, are simultaneously engaged in the overlapping processes of state and nation building. While these two processes have "historical and logical connections," the nation building puts emphasis on the attainment of a common consciousness (Finer 1975, 88). In other words, "a society," as the sociologist Louis Wirth (1936, xxv) once put it, "is possible" when "individuals in it carry around in their heads some sort of picture of that society." Wartime experiences or sufferings can be utilized to "invent" traditions (Hobsbawm 1983) or "imagine" political communities (Anderson 2006).

The PKK movement, in contrast to nearly all past Kurdish nationalist uprisings that included tribal, regional, and/or religious elements, aims at forging a broad-based modern and secular Kurdish identity. The emphasis on "remaking" Kurdish identity, as evidenced by the proclamation to create new men and women noted in chapter 3, has greatly helped to subdue and overcome parochial loyalties and identities and create a new civic Kurdish identity that cuts across the regional, religious, and tribal lines that heavily influenced earlier Kurdish rebellions. The PKK, as Romano (2006, 161) observed, has "altered the cultural tool kit of Kurds in Turkey."

The PKK, along with a number of sociopolitical organizations it has created or inspired, has seized opportunities in events ranging from funerals of fallen militants, to the Newroz festivals celebrating the beginning of spring, to weddings parties, and to setting up alternative Friday prayers to disseminate its message and educate the masses. The invocation and reinterpretation of Newroz as a contemporary myth—reinventing it as a reference to the antiquity of the Kurdish nation and its rich culture and equating it with contemporary resistance for national liberation—has played a key role in the PKK's success in recreating or reinventing traditions in that it situates the PKK in a historical narrative and helps forge a national identity (Gunes 2012, 2013).

In addition to such an emphasis on the need to "remake" Kurdish identity, war dynamics have greatly influenced ordinary Kurds identifying with a broad-based modern Kurdish identity. The protracted armed conflict has paved the way for the rise of a common consciousness. This shared pain and suffering and the ensuing histories have created collective forms of meaning and helped bring millions of ordinary Kurds together, facilitating the construction of a new political community (Hutchison 2016). Kurdishness, as the former mayor cited in the previous chapter noted, has been a key outcome of three decades of armed conflict. A vast majority of subjects interviewed pointed out that the armed conflict has made them "more aware of their Kurdish identity" and that they have become "more cognizant of their sociopolitical environment" as a result of the conflict.

The nation-building aspect of the PKK movement is not limited to the hard-core supporters, "constituents," or "adherents." Even bystanders or observers, such as devout Kurdish Muslims who distance themselves from the PKK due in part to its secular ideology, give credit to the PKK insurgency for forging or remaking Kurdishness. Gurses (2015b), based on in-depth interviews with conservative Kurdish religious groups, reports that more than two-thirds of total respondents acknowledged the effect of armed conflict on becoming more aware of their Kurdish identity.

The response from a pious male interviewee in his seventies illustrates how the armed conflict has helped weaken traditional elements in Kurdishness and forge a new political identity. This interviewee, who was arrested for his involvement with the PKK and refusal to ally with the state against them in the 1990s, emphatically argued that "we, Sunni Kurds and Yezidi Kurds, all are a part of the same nation regardless of our religious differences."

The Yazidis are a Kurmanji-speaking group with a syncretic religion that includes elements from Zoroastrianism as well as Islam, Christianity, Judaism, and Shamanism. They have historically been discriminated against, and since the early nineteenth century have faced continuous and systematic massacres at the hands of the Ottomans, who were often allied with Muslim Kurds (Jwaideh 2006, 20). Consistent with the definition of political culture used in this book that emphasizes the significance of "shared culture," many Muslim Kurds have begun to embrace the Yazidis as their Kurdish brethren despite religious differences.

The dialectical nature of nationalism, which requires the ethnic, cultural, or religious "other," is brought to the forefront by three decades of armed conflict between two groups hailing from the same faith. While the conflict between Muslim Turks and Kurds has resulted in questioning the value of Islam that crosscuts ethnicity, an outcome that I discuss extensively in the next chapter, the same war dynamics have facilitated the rise of a newly defined Kurdish identity inclusive of non-Muslim Yazidi Kurds. This shared vision, an imagined community of Kurds, is likely to leave a lasting legacy of resistance.

Conclusion

This chapter examines the connection between war and political culture. Building on the Kurdish case, it demonstrates that wartime experiences disrupt traditional social culture often characterized by silence and deference to authority. War situations help participants break the barrier of fear, empower hidden strengths, and engender a dissident political culture. Results from this chapter contribute to and support earlier studies that have pointed out positive political outcomes of war using such cases as El Salvador (Wood 2003), Uganda (Blattman 2009), and Sierra Leone (Bellows and Miguel 2009).

In addition to an increased political participation, war dynamics also pushed for the logic of equality (an intrinsic component of democracy) and engendered norms and attitudes that are favorable to democracy at the micro level. The results demonstrate that civil war experiences could facilitate the rise of a more inclusive and participatory democratic culture. Consistent with the social-psychological mechanism outlined in the theory chapter, wartime experiences help the sufferer to connect on a special level of mutual understanding that makes them particularly empathetic toward the marginalized groups. As an interviewee put it, her experiences in the conflict zone helped her to develop empathy for members of other, smaller minorities. She also pointed out that she has become more tolerant of different views and opinions, a cardinal virtue of democratic culture (Gibson 1988; Booth and Seligson 2009).

This new sense of personal worth, dignity, and assertiveness from wartime experiences has laid the groundwork for the rise of individuals with a sense of empowerment and responsibility. The Kurdish insurgent group, through such notions as "democratic autonomy," enabled ordinary Kurds to participate in local assemblies of self-rule and decision making. These programs and institutions, which are essentially outcomes of the armed conflict, have created a social space within which ordinary Kurdish men and women have begun to partake in decision making at the societal level. This approach, which "revives a communal and federalist tradition" with an emphasis on "active citizenship and connectivity" (Jongerden 2017, 257), is akin to what Arendt (1990) refers to as space of freedom: the creation of public platforms that enable people as free and equal citizens who take their common concerns into their own hands. The American political activist Meredith Tax (2016a, 155) likens these programs to community organization or neighborhood councils that constitute an import aspect of American democracy at the local level.

Finally, the PKK insurgency has resulted in the rise of a newly defined Kurdish political community. War dynamics, along with the insurgent group's relentless efforts to remake Kurdish identity, have greatly reshaped Kurdishness. The PKK movement and armed conflict have successfully transformed traditional, nonpolitical Kurdish masses into Kurds who are well aware of their Kurdishness. Thus, if one might borrow the well-known observation of nineteenth-century Italian statesman Massimo d'Azeglio, "we have made Italy: now we must make Italians," one could point out that Kurds have been made but now must make a country.

## FIVE

War and Religion

Due partly to the complex and ineffable nature of religion, research into the specific influence of religious factors on conflict has produced inconclusive findings. In a detailed examination of the roles religion played in the Sierra Leonean civil war, Conteh (2011, 55) argues against "singular modalities of religion" and draws attention to how religion played as "instigator," "justifier," and finally "reconciler" during and after the war. Thus, while religion's salience to ethnic identity and conflict varies (Fox 1997, 6), two main approaches can be identified: religion is used by political entrepreneurs to highlight existing societal cleavages and exacerbate conflicts, or religion bridges ethnic divides and helps build peace. This is mainly because religious tradition is "never a single, unchanging essence that impels people to act in a uniform way" (Armstrong 2014, 123). In other words, as Soleimani (2016, 25) notes, religions "are susceptible to different readings in different contexts and become entangled in or influenced by newer sociopolitical context."

Echoing Juergensmeyer's (2017, 5) argument of the "odd attraction of religion and violence," a group of studies highlights the violent nature of religion in civil wars. This effect is of particular interest when religious identities overlap with ethnic boundaries. Gubler and Selway (2012) find that ethnicity substantially increases the probability of civil war onset when it is reinforced by other salient social cleavages such as religion and socioeconomic class. When religion is an integral component of an ethnic identity, it can become a readily available instrument for political entrepreneurs to exploit. In these situations (e.g., Southerners in Sudan until 2005;

Chechens in Russia), religion exacerbates tensions and deepens ethnic divisions. The overlap of religion and ethnicity, two of the most salient social cleavages, have been found to increase the risk of the onset of war (Basedau et al. 2011), result in longer and deadlier conflicts (Toft 2007), and undermine prospects for a peaceful solution (Svensson 2007).

This characterization of religion and violence, however, has not gone without challenge. Drawing attention to "the seeds of tolerance, justice, compassion, and peace" in religious traditions, a number of studies argue that religion can help bring about peace and democracy (Johansen 1997, 53; Driessen 2010, 2014). Religion, in the words of Philpott (2007, 505), "devastates not only New York skyscrapers but also authoritarian regimes; it constructs not only bellicose communal identities but also democratic civil society." Religious groups can mediate between the protagonists, help keep the lines of communication open, and reduce the suspicion and negative perceptions that accompany deteriorating relations in times of war (Sampson 1994; Toft, Philpott, and Shah 2011; Sandal 2011; Goldberg 2016). Appleby (2000, 238) highlights the potential for religious actors playing a constructive and transformative role in peace building and argues that religious leaders can gradually "saturate" the society by transforming the conflict environment and condemning violence to foster crosscommunal cooperation.

Nonetheless, when political considerations take precedence, religious leaders and authorities might no longer be perceived as legitimate or neutral in conflict situations (Haynes 2009). Despite religion's potential as a peacemaker noted above, "the political, economic, and security dimensions of most social confrontations usually outweigh" that of the religious as the considerations of realpolitik kick in (Johnston 1994, 263). Gurses and Rost (2016) empirically examine these alternative propositions using a global sample of ethnic civil wars that started and ended between 1950 and 2006. While they do not reject the possibility of religion serving as a peacemaker, they conclude that the subordination of religion to national interests in the context of war negates the hypothesized positive effect of religion on peace duration in the aftermath of ethnic civil wars. This is particularly relevant in cases where both the ethnic rebels and government hail from the same faith, as national identities are prioritized at the expense of religion, rendering common faith an ineffective peacemaker.

In this chapter, I examine how war dynamics diminish the significance of religion as a common denominator and specify how armed conflict between two ethnic groups that share the same faith can reduce the role religion plays in ethnonationalist identity. What dynamics are at work when the warring groups are of the same faith? How does religion turn into an instrument of legitimation and mobilization in the hands of political entrepreneurs? How does ethnic conflict influence minority groups' attitudes toward religion? Drawing on the Kurdish conflict in Turkey, I address these questions and demonstrate the secularizing potential of ethnic armed conflict.

Islam as an Instrument of Assimilation against the Kurds

Islam has long served as a tool of oppression and assimilation at the hands of the Turkish state. It was used to distinguish Muslim masses from non-Muslim Armenians and Greeks in the early twentieth century then to justify their exclusion, deportation, or expulsion. It was also used to mobilize Muslim Turks and Kurds against Greek, French, and British invaders during the War of Independence in the 1920s. While it was relegated to a secondary position in the newly forged Turkish national identity after the formation of modern Turkey, the state employed it to assimilate Kurds into Turkish culture.

The Directorate of Religious Affairs (Diyanet Isleri Baskanligi), which was instituted in 1924 to bring religion under state control, used an army of state-appointed prayer leaders (imams) serving at mosques throughout the country to spread a state-approved brand of Islam. While the nascent Turkish state utilized the directorate to pacify Islamist movements, it also used Islam to Turkify the large Kurdish minority in the East. Weekly sermons were delivered in Turkish regardless of whether the congregation actually spoke the language (in most cases it did not). Imams were instructed to follow the state-sanctioned Hanafi school of Islam even though the majority of Kurds adhered to the Shafi school.

This utilitarian view of Islam can be traced back to the mid-nineteenth century, when the Ottoman elites used a Turkish-Islamic discourse to justify Ottoman Turkish rule over non-Muslim Bulgarians and Armenians as well as Muslim Kurds and Arabs. As Soleimani (2016, chaps. 4–5) argues at length, such a reconstruction of Turkish identity in which Islam played an instrumental role dislodged Islam from the Arabic culture and nationalized the religion.

The establishment of a modern, secular Turkey in 1923 by Mustafa Kemal Ataturk saw Islam become less visible while still maintaining an important role in creating a national identity. Ziya Gokalp, who is credited for greatly influencing the nationalist sentiments of Kemal Ataturk, underlines the significance of upbringing, language, and religion over other aspects of nationalism (Yanarocak 2014). The reduced status assigned to Islam in the new Turkish identity was also partly driven by the fact that non-Muslim subjects were almost entirely absent. By the 1930s, the population of Turkey mostly consisted of Muslim Turks and Kurds. Therefore, the new Turkish elite embarked on a nation-building project centered on Turkification with a redefined, nationalized role for religion to integrate an ethnic group that would otherwise clash with the dominant nationalist climate.

Thus, while the Kemalist state introduced radical social reforms aimed at secularization of Turkish political culture, it also emulated the Ottoman utilitarian approach to Islam in order to suppress Kurdish dissent in the East. Despite the Kemalist elites' disdain for anything religious, the Turkish state was not only reluctant to suppress Sufi religious fraternities (*tarikats*) in the Kurdish region, but it also encouraged religious revival by providing Kurdish religious leaders (*sheikhs*) with both material and moral support (McDowall 2004, 399; also see van Bruinessen 1999, 19).

The state also gave wide latitude to Islamic communities and groups (Islami Cemaatler) to operate in the Kurdish-dominated East, especially after the 1980 military coup. As Yanarocak (2016) explains at great length, the adoption of the Turkish-Islam Synthesis as the core state ideology gained momentum after the September 12, 1980 military takeover. General Kenan Evren, the leader of the coup, defended and supported the use of Islam as the glue of the nation. Significantly, he advocated using Islam to unite non-Turkish citizens. Evren stated, "despite the fact that we recognize some of our citizens as Turks, they (Kurds) do not accept this. Then we can use Islam for that. . . . Can't we realize unity and togetherness by regaining these fooled people [Kurds] with religion?" (Oran 2006, 251–52, cited in Yanarocak 2016, 146).

In the 1990s, during which the secular Turkish army orchestrated the overthrow of a coalition government dominated by the Islamist Welfare Party on the grounds that it was becoming a center for antisecular activities, the Turkish state either ignored or encouraged the violent Islamist Kurdish Hizbullah to engage in a brutal feud with the PKK. It should be mentioned that this group bears no relation to the Lebanese Shi'a militia. Partially thanks to the Turkish authorities' implicit consent for its bloody campaign against the PKK, Hizbullah managed to establish itself in the Kurdish majority provinces of Diyarbakir, Batman, and Mardin that were known for strongly supporting the PKK. When hostilities ceased between the two groups and the government captured the PKK's Abdullah Ocalan in 1999, Turkish police raided a house in Istanbul and killed Hizbullah's leader. The Kurdish Islamists then came under constant state pressure, resulting in the arrest of more than five thousand suspected members in less than two years (Cakir 2007).[1]

Hizbullah was absent from the public eye in the early 2000s, but it resurfaced later under a legal association, the Association for the Oppressed (Mustazaflar Dernegi). In 2012 it formed the Free Cause Party (Hur Dava Partisi, HudaPar) to challenge the pro-Kurdish Peace and Democracy Party (BDP) in the East.[2] Similar to previous secular center-right or center-left governments turning a blind eye on the group in order to weaken the PKK in the 1990s, the Islamist AKP tolerated such resurfacing. While this was due in part to the AKP's Islamist identity, Hizbullah was also seen as a useful instrument to undermine the PKK's influence.

While there is a "striking continuity between the Kemalist and post-Kemalist Turkey" in its handling of the Kurdish problem (Neuberger 2014, 27), the AKP resorted to Islam to appeal to the Kurdish public to a degree that was never seen before. The aforementioned Directorate of Religious Affairs, for instance, has effectively turned into a party apparatus under AKP rule to reinforce the state-sanctioned Islam and promote and spread Turkish nationalism (Ozturk 2016, 632–33).

In line with the AKP's goal of "raising pious generations" (Cengiz 2014), the number of religious high schools (Imam Hatip) and students enrolled in these schools have seen a recent increase throughout Turkey. A limited number of Imam Hatip schools were originally established to train Islamic clerics and preachers in the late 1940s. Their numbers gradually increased and they transformed into schools that specialized in religious education combined with a modern curriculum. Following the 1997 military intervention that forced the Islamic Welfare Party–dominated government from power, the newly formed centrist government enforced age restrictions for pupils and prevented graduates from studying subjects other than theology at university (Gundogan and Baillon 2014). These measures significantly reduced their numbers from 612 schools during the 1998–99 school year to 450 by 2002–3 school year (Makovsky 2015).

Since the rise of the AKP in November 2002, the ban on Imam Hatip schools has been scrapped and scholarships have been offered to thousands for enrollment. Regular schools have been converted into Imam Hatip schools, and students who scored low marks have been assigned to these schools by the Ministry of Education. These policies have led to a significant increase in both the number of religious high schools and the number of students enrolled. As of the 2015–16 academic year, 677,205 students were enrolled at 1,149 senior (*lise*) Imam Hatip schools across the country.[3]

Data from the Ministry of Education shows that Kurdish provinces have significantly lower levels of education when compared to the rest of the country, but provinces with a significant Kurdish population rank higher in the number of Imam Hatip high schools.[4] Kurdish provinces are receiving more religious education than provinces with majority-Turkish populations. As presented in table 11, notwithstanding significantly lower levels of schooling ratio (66.16 percent in Kurdish-populated provinces vs. 85.01 percent in majority-Turkish provinces) and number of regular high schools per 100,000 (13.01 vs. 14.60), Kurdish provinces have significantly higher rate of Imam Hatip schools (2.17 vs. 1.85). They also have a significantly higher ratio of population enrolled in these schools (.012 percent versus .008 percent).[5]

The electoral victory of the AKP has wrought many radical changes. It has brought the previously excluded Muslim Turkish masses and Islamists to power and weakened the self-appointed guardian of the Kemalist republic, the staunchly secular Turkish army. It has also paved the way for an overall Islamization of society.

With respect to the Kurdish conflict, the AKP and its Islamist allies long blamed the existence of the problem on the secular nationalism embraced by Kemalists, and they resorted to the Islamic brotherhood thesis as a supra identity for all. This platform would serve as a cure for the armed conflict. The approach is encapsulated in the words of Turkish president Tayyip Erdogan, who has repeatedly made references to Islam as an overarching identity and stated that whenever anyone asks one about one's identity, one should simply respond that "I am Muslim, that is enough."[6]

The AKP has been eager to de-emphasize secular Turkish nationalism only to have promoted an Islamized version. While the Kemalist

TABLE 11. Religious Education in the Kurdish Regions of Turkey, 2015

Variable	Kurdish Regions (Mean)	Rest of the Country (Mean)	Difference (Sig. Level)
Net schooling ratio (high school)	66.16	85.01	−18.86 (<.001)
# of high schools per 100,000 people (Imam Hatip high schools excluded)	13.01	14.60	−1.65 (.08)
# of Imam Hatip high schools per 100,000 people	2.17	1.85	.31 (.08)
% total population enrolled in Imam Hatip high schools	.012	.008	.0037 (.001)

Note: Significance levels are based on two-sided *t*-tests assuming unequal variance.

elites encouraged Kurds to assimilate into Turkish society by eschewing their own culture, the Islamists support a type of Turkish nationalism that encourages Kurds to ignore their culture and assimilate as Muslims. Despite the rhetoric of Islamic brotherhood, there has been no substantive departure from the past. For example, even though Islam is an identity that supposedly ignores ethnic and linguistic differences, calls for Friday sermons to be held in Kurdish in Kurdish-majority provinces are still deemed as a threat to Turkish unity and national interest.

Below I first offer an argument for how ethnic conflict between coreligionists paves the way for secularization by suppressing the role of religion in ethnic identity construction. Next, building on survey data and interviews with dozens of Kurds, I show how the subordination of Islam to Turkish national interests interacts with the three-decade insurgency, resulting in many Kurds re-examining the role of Islam in their identity.

Armed Conflict, Ethnicity, and Religion

Identity formation is complex and contextual. Ethnic identities are fluid and interact with a set of social, economic, and political processes (Fearon and Laitin 2000; Brubaker 2009). Bormann, Cederman, and Vogt (2017) in their examination of linguistic and religious differences, two salient cleavages that are often considered bases of ethnic identity, find that linguistic cleavages are a better predictor of civil war onset than religious differences. This effect, they argue, depends on regional context; it is more pronounced in eastern Europe and Asia than the rest of the world. Posner (2004), exploring the conditions under which social and cultural cleavages become politically relevant, reaches a similar conclusion and finds that identities can be more or less salient at different points in time or in different countries. Tejel (2016, 259) highlights the dynamic nature of majority-minority relations and argues that ethnic identities are subject to a dynamic process in which these identities are constantly negotiated. Both individual and collective identities "can be 'activated' or 'deactivated' within the political field depending on the context, the needs, and the subjectivity of the actors involved."

In cases where religion is a marker that differentiates groups from one another, religious identity is likely to be pronounced and strengthened as a result of armed conflict. The overlap of ethnic and religious identities can change the very nature of a war and transform a secular conflict into a religious one, as demonstrated by the Palestinians vs. Israel or Kashmir vs. India (Fox 2000; Zeb 2006). But in societies where religion is shared by both combatants, as in the case of Kurds vs. Turkey, armed conflict is more likely to strengthen ethnic identity at the expense of religious identity.

This convergence of ethnicity and religion might, as Gubler and Selway (2012) argue, diminish the risk of war through altering the costs of rebellion and shaping issues. Though religion might serve as a moderator, the outbreak of war creates a fundamentally different environment with different goals and priorities. As Harpviken and Roislien (2008, 359) note, "regardless of whether or not religion was part of the complex of causes starting a war, the significance of religion will be altered as a result of conflict."

In the process of defining its place in the system, an ethnic minority will emphasize its differences, not commonalities, with the dominant group. This process of "identity differentiation" is likely to result in the reconstruction of an ethnic identity in which religion is a subordinate factor (Aspinall 2007, 2009). Coupled with the politicization of religion, which turns it into an instrument to bolster the warring groups' agendas, armed conflict reinforces ethnic identity at the expense of religious identity. Faith as a common denominator, the glue that binds coreligionists, turns into another contested field as groups strive to utilize it for their own agendas.

The Acehnese rebellion in Indonesia is an example of this transformation. The politicization of religion—its use by the dominant Javanese to pacify Acehnese opposition—resulted in the Acehnese gradually abandoning the Islamism, which played a key role in the rebellion of the 1950s. As the Indonesian state appealed to coreligiosity to weaken the separatist movement, the Acehnese began to see Muslim, Indonesian, and Acehnese identities as distinct fields with boundaries that did not necessarily coincide (Aspinall 2009, 20). Consequently the Acehnese opposition, a movement with deep religious roots, was transformed into a secessionist movement with secular goals by the end of the next cycle of rebellion in the 2000s (Aspinall 2009, 11).

Ethnic civil war in which protagonists are of the same religion creates social spaces conducive to secularization because the conflict weakens the ability of religious authorities to claim a moral high ground. They then lose their ability to shape mass views on what make up true religion. The politicization of religion in the context of ethnic civil war helps forge a "nationalized" religious identity in which religion loses its significance as the dominant force. While it may still play a role in identity formation, faith loses its role as the dominant frame of reference. Ethical relativism and individualism, two important aspects of secularization (Dobbelaere

1999, 2002; Norris and Inglehart 2004), are likely to emerge, leading to multiple and contending interpretations of religion.

An Empirical Look at the War-Secularization Nexus

Before I test this secularization hypothesis against 2,100 individual wartime experiences, it should be stated that secularization is a multidimensional concept and has been the subject of an extensive and heated debate. Taylor (2011, 37–38), in his analysis of the Western march to secularity, identifies two closely related vectors. First, it involves a move toward "a more personal, committed, and inward form of religion," which can be described as the privatization of religion. The shift also includes "the repression of 'magical' elements in religion." This movement involves a disenchanted world in which superstitions give way to science to explain the universe. In a similar vein, Casanova (2011) points to increasing structural differentiation of religion and politics (institutional differentiation), the privatization of religion, and the progressive decline of the social significance of religious beliefs and practices as three core dimensions of secularization.

Dobbelaere (2002, 24–25) dissects the term and distinguishes between three levels of secularization. First, societal secularization broadly denotes a functional differentiation process by which religion loses its overarching claims and is reduced to one system among many. Second, organizational secularization expresses change occurring in the posture of religious organizations (religious change). Finally, individual secularization indicates individual behavior and measures the degree of normative integration in religious bodies (religious involvement).

To be sure, secularization is multilayered and addressing all aspects of it is well beyond the scope of this study. I use the term "secularization" to refer to a general tendency toward a world in which religion matters less (Calhoun, Juergensmeyer, and VanAntwerpen 2011, 10). In other words, secularization involves religious decline; "a systemic erosion of religious practices, values, and beliefs" (Norris and Inglehart 2004, 5). The theory outlined above addresses how war experiences impact individuals' attitudes toward religion. Thus "individual secularization" or "privatization of religion" is of particular interest and is the focus of the following analysis.

I used responses to four questions and statements to gauge individual secularization as defined above. Responses to the question, "How important is religion in your life?" take values ranging from "1" (not at all important),

"2" (not very important), "3" (rather important), to "4" (very important). The next question was aimed at measuring mosque attendance. Responses to "How often do you pray at mosque?" can take values ranging from "1" (never), "2" (once a week), "3" (a few times a week), to "4" (every day).

While mosque attendance can be an important indicator of individual piety, daily prayer might constitute a stronger indicator of zeal. Other than the weekly Friday mass, Islam does not require mosque attendance but orders its followers to pray five times a day. Toward this end, subjects were asked to answer the question, "Do you regularly pray five times a day?" with responses taking values "1" (Yes) and "0" (No).

Finally, responses to another statement were used to assess the degree of breaking out of superstitions and becoming more secular. Participants were asked to express agreement or disagreement with the following statement: "Whenever science and religion conflict, religion is always right," which can consist of values "1" (strongly disagree), "2" (disagree), "3" (agree), and "4" (strongly agree).

An analysis of the data shows that religion plays an important role in participants' lives. Nearly 60 percent of the 2,100 respondents from three Kurdish provinces in which the survey was conducted stated that religion is "very important" in their lives. More than half said that they pray regularly, and about one-third stated that they attend mosque at least once a week. Regarding the statement that "whenever science and religion conflict, religion is always right," a slight majority, 52 percent, agreed with this statement while about 35 percent of the respondents "strongly disagreed" or "disagreed." These results point to an important variation despite the conservative social structure prevalent in Kurdish society.

What remains to be seen is whether wartime experiences can help explain this variation. How does exposure to violence relate to a decline in religiosity? As presented in table 12, self-identified victims of conflict-related violence are markedly less religious and have more negative attitudes toward religion when compared to those who are not. Religion plays a lesser role in the lives of respondents who experienced violence because of the armed conflict.

The negative signs on the coefficients for the exposure to violence index indicate that an increase in the values of this variable results in less religiosity. Specifically, one standard deviation increase in the value of the exposure to violence index decreases the odds of religion playing an important role in participants' lives by 30 percent (model 1). Similarly, the effect of exposure to violence on mosque attendance is noticeable (model 2). One standard deviation increase in exposure to violence results in an 18 percent decrease in the odds of mosque attendance.

Results from a logistic regression using an alternative measure of religious participation confirm the demonstrable effect of war experiences on secularization. As presented in model 3, those subjects that have been exposed to violence are significantly less likely to pray five times a day. To estimate the magnitude of the effect of war experiences on the probability of praying five times a day, I converted the logit estimates into predicted probabilities. A change in the value of exposure to violence index from "0" (no exposure) to "1" (maximum exposure), while holding other variables at their means, decreases the predicted probability of "daily prayer" by 0.35.

Responses to the fourth statement used to measure secularization paint a similar picture. Exposure to violence is significantly and negatively associated with agreeing with the statement, "Whenever science and religion conflict, religion is always right" (model 4). One standard deviation

TABLE 12. Armed Conflict and Attitudes toward Religion

Variable	Model 1	Model 2	Model 3	Model 4
	Importance of Religion	Mosque Attendance	Daily Prayer	Religion vs. Science
Exposure to Violence	-1.47***	-.83***	-1.50***	-1.79***
Index	[.19]	[.19]	[.19]	[.20]
Sex	-.69***	-3.09***	-.05	-.86***
	[.10]	[.15]	[.10]	[.09]
Age	-.09	.22***	.14**	-.13***
	[.06]	[.05]	[.06]	[.05]
Education	-.41***	-.15***	-.28***	-.45***
	[.06]	[.05]	[.05]	[.06]
Automobile	.11	.04	.06	.01
	[.09]	[.09]	[.09]	[.09]
# of Children	.12***	-.01	.17***	.06***
	[.03]	[.02]	[.03]	[.02]
Constant			.33	
			[.26]	
Cut 1	-6.15	-1.25		-5.33
Cut 2	-4.37	.50		-2.84
Cut 3	-1.93	2.41		-.13
N	2100	2100	2100	2100
Pseudo R^2	.06	.17	.10	.05
Prob.>Chi^2	<.001	<.001	<.001	<.001

Note: ** significant at 5 percent level; *** significant at 1 percent level (two-tailed). Robust standard errors in brackets.

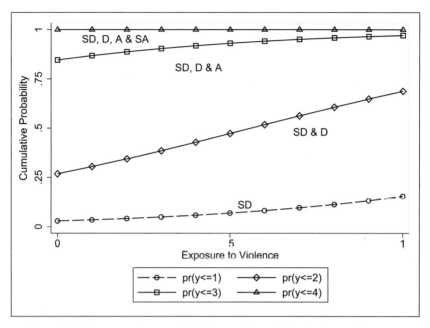

Figure 10. Whenever science and religion conflict, religion is always right

increase in the value of exposure to violence index decreases the odds of agreeing with this statement by 35.7 percent.

This effect is visualized in figure 10, using the responses to the statement, "Whenever science and religion conflict, religion is always right." The cumulative probability for "strongly disagree" (SD) and "disagree" (D) responses reveals a strong positive correlation with the exposure to violence index.

Of the control variables, those for education and sex are associated with negative attitudes toward religion, whereas having more children, often deemed a sign of traditional societies, is significantly and positively associated with supportive attitudes toward religion. The effect of exposure to violence, the main independent variable, is as robust as that of education, arguably the most powerful predictor of individual modernity (Inkeles and Smith 1974).

Accounting for the Insurgent Group's Ideology

While the results presented above indicate a strong relationship between wartime violence and changing attitudes toward religion, the analysis does not control for the effect of ideology on the outcome. This is of particular importance given the PKK's secular ideology and its overall left-oriented approach that dismisses religion as "a veil of conservatism and ignorance" and an instrument of domination in the hands of those who oppress the Kurds (Romano 2006, 134).

To be sure, Islam as a potent force has compelled the secular Kurdish national movement to soften its stance toward religion. In the 1990s, the PKK leader Ocalan, in his *A Revolutionary Approach to the Question of Religion* (*Din Sorununa Devrimci Bakis*), pointed to the necessity of utilizing religion against the state and its collaborators. As a result of this strategy, the PKK reached out to Kurdish religious figures and formed organizations such as the Union of Patriotic Imams of Kurdistan (Kurdistan Yurtsever Imamlar Birligi) and the Islamic Party of Kurdistan (Kurdistan Islam Partisi) (see, for instance, McDowall 2004). In 2011 the pro-Kurdish Peace and Democracy Party (BDP) called on its supporters to boycott Friday mass prayers at government-controlled mosques. Instead, it urged Muslim Kurds to attend alternative Friday prayers led by Kurdish imams as part of a civil disobedience campaign against government policies toward the Kurds (Sarigil and Fazlioglu 2013).

Nonetheless, although the PKK has adopted a more accommodative attitude toward Islam (Bruinessen 1999), its overall approach to religion has remained true to an ideology rooted in Marxist doctrine. The PKK leader Ocalan (2012, 34) still describes sheikdom and sectarianism as parasitic institutions, vestiges of the Middle Ages that are obstacles to democratization. The PKK may recognize religion as a necessary evil, but it is still a thoroughly secular organization. In the words of one observer, the PKK is arguably "the most important secular insurgent political movement in the Middle East" (Jongerden 2016, 107).

Does accounting for the PKK's ideology enhance negative attitudes toward religion? How does the insurgent group's secular ideology interact with wartime experiences in producing a secular culture? To isolate the effect of violence on the outcome, I re-examined the interplay between armed conflict, ideology, and secularization by adding the measures of ideology used in previous chapters. A number of important conclusions can be drawn from the findings presented in table 13.

Controlling for ideology by itself does not lead to a substantial change in the war-religion relationship. As shown in model 1, respondents who experienced violence are more likely to view religion as a "less important" element in their lives even after removing the effect of the ideology variable from the outcome. The effect of exposure to violence on having negative views of religion was discernible regardless of how the outcome variable was measured (not shown).

The impact of ideology is not only noticeable but also manifold. It has an independent and direct effect on the outcome. Respondents who voted for the Kurdish political party are significantly more likely than those who did not to hold negative attitudes toward religion. This effect is robust across all five models. The BDP supporters are less likely to view religion as "important" (models 1 and 2), attend mosque (model 3), and pray daily (model 4). They are also less likely to agree with the statement, "When science and religion conflict, religion is always right" (model 5).

TABLE 13. Violence, Ideology, and Religion

Variable	Model 1	Model 2	Model 3	Model 4	Model 5
	Importance of Religion		Mosque Attendance	Daily Prayer	Religion vs. Science
Exposure to Violence Index	−.89*** [.23]	−.31 [.33]	−1.17*** [.03]	−.30 [.32]	−.37 [.28]
Voted for the BDP	−.59*** [.10]	−.41*** [.12]	−.67*** [.10]	−.29** [.12]	−.49*** [.12]
Exposure* BDP		−1.02** [.42]	.05 [.39]	−1.05*** [.41]	−.30 [.39]
State as Perpetrator	−.17 [.11]	−.15 [.11]	−.30*** [.11]	−.33*** [.12]	.06 [.11]
Rebels as Perpetrator	.45*** [.16]	.44*** [.16]	−.06 [.12]	.10 [.15]	.08 [.14]
Sex	−.63*** [.19]	−.62*** [.10]	−.77*** [.09]	.009 [.10]	−3.07*** [.14]
Age	−.14** [.05]	−.14*** [.05]	−.18*** [.05]	.10* [.06]	.19*** [.05]
Education	−.38*** [.05]	−.38*** [.05]	−.43*** [.06]	−.26*** [.06]	−.15*** [.05]
Automobile	.05 [.09]	.06 [.09]	−.04 [.08]	.02 [.09]	.01 [.09]
# of Children	.13*** [.03]	.13*** [.03]	.07*** [.02]	.18*** [.03]	−.01 [.02]
Constant				.51** [.26]	
Cut 1	−6.40	−6.39	−5.71		−1.44
Cut 2	−4.60	−4.59	−3.17		.33
Cut 3	−2.11	−2.09	−.40		2.25
N	2100	2100	2100	2100	2100
Pseudo R^2	.07	.07	.06	.11	.17
Prob.>Chi^2	<.001	<.001	<.001	<.001	<.001

Note: * significant at 10 percent level; ** significant at 5 percent level; *** significant at 1 percent level (two-tailed). Robust standard errors in brackets.

Although the effect of exposure to violence still significantly predicts attitudes toward religion, its effect is noticeably weakened when an interaction term between violence and ideology is added to the analysis. The role ideology plays in producing negative attitudes toward religion appears to be strong and multifaceted. The main effect of wartime experiences on producing less religiosity varies for the BDP and non-BDP supporters, as demonstrated by the coefficients on the interaction term (Exposure*BDP) in models 2 and 4. The significant negative effect of violence on rendering religion "less important" (model 2) and lowering the chances of daily prayer (model 4) appears to work through the ideology.

Based on model 4, figure 11 visualizes how violence interacts with ideology. Wartime experiences impact those who support the BDP (the proxy used for ideology) differently than those who do not. Given that the Kurdish population is basically split between pro-Kurdish parties and the ruling AKP, these findings effectively explain differences between BDP and AKP voters as they face armed conflict. Such a split also confirms key differences between two primary parties in the Kurdish region with drastically different ideologies and views of religion. While the AKP supporters' attitudes toward daily prayer do not change much as they are exposed to violence, the probability of daily prayer diminishes greatly for BDP supporters as a result of their experiences with bloodshed.

Consistent with the findings obtained earlier, respondents who think the state is at fault for the conflict (and their suffering) are more likely to develop negative attitudes toward religion. They attend mosque less frequently and are less likely to pray daily (models 3 and 4). In models 1 and 2, Kurds who blame the rebels for the violence are significantly more likely to ascribe greater importance to religion. Furthermore, in confirmation of the argument that those who experienced violence firsthand are more likely to experience sociopolitical change, alternative model specifications showed that those who were directly exposed to violence were more likely to hold negative attitudes toward religion (not shown).

Evidence from Qualitative Data

As noted in the introduction, the survey data provides a snapshot of the overall relationship between the main explanatory and outcome variables. To better address this important case and describe the mechanisms through which war experiences result in secularization, I now present evidence from face-to-face interviews with individuals born and raised in the

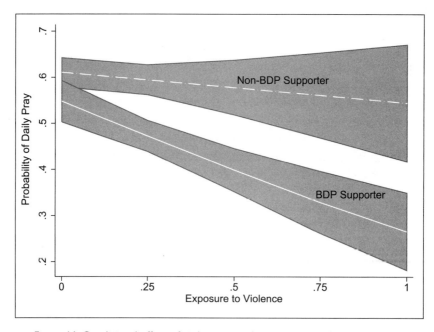

Figure 11. Conditional effect of violence on religion

Kurdish region of Turkey. Evidence from these lengthy interviews with individuals whose lives were directly affected by the conflict sheds further light on the asserted relationship between wartime dynamics and individual secularization. In contrast to the random sample presented above, special care was given to have a group that included a diverse set of individuals to better examine the secularizing impact of decades-long armed conflict. Significantly, this sample of eleven female and twenty-nine male interviewees ranging from twenty-three to seventy-five years of age includes a broad range of Kurds but excludes those from secular backgrounds to better assess the link between conflict and religion. Of these forty subjects, 35 percent had no formal education, 10 percent received primary school education, and only 27.5 percent of them had a college degree.

Two general findings emerged. In confirmation of the argument that religion as a potent force is likely to turn into an instrument of legitimization, one group argued that Islam has been used by the Turkish state to suppress the Kurdish movement. Islam, this group contended, is being "misused" and "misinterpreted" by the dominant Turks to undermine Kurdish demands for equal rights. A pious, sixty-year-old farmer expressed frustration and anger at President Erdogan for holding the Muslim holy book at election rallies. Referring to Turkish president Erdogan waving a copy of the Qur'an during election rallies in several Kurdish-dominated provinces before the 2015 general elections, he argued that "this is not where our holy book belongs. Erdogan is abusing Islam for his own political interests."

Several subjects voiced a similar view and criticized the Turkish government for using religion for its political interests. A forty-one-year old lawyer lamented that "of course this is not Islam. But its use as an instrument against the Kurds has resulted in questioning religion itself, especially among the youth." This "moral decay," he maintained, is a direct result of "many Kurds equating Islam with the Turkish state policies."

Additionally, those who claimed that Islam is being abused by the government also stated that religion should not be a part of the political game. A school teacher in his thirties, a practicing Muslim, said that he has come to the conclusion that "religion is a matter between man and God." Thus, the interviewees have not only started questioning the relationship between religion and politics by distinguishing the secular spheres from religious institutions and norms [what Casanova (2011) termed institutional differentiation], but have also gone through a transformation that has turned religion into a personal matter (religious privatization).

Another primary finding was that consistent use of Islam as a weapon against Kurdish demands for equal treatment has resulted in a systematic erosion of religious beliefs and practices, or religious decline. A devout Muslim school teacher in his mid-thirties confessed that he felt "disaffected toward religion" by events in recent years, particularly "the resistance from his Muslim Turkish brethren to Kurdish rightful demands for equality." A twenty-three-year-old college dropout, in reference to Islam being used against the Kurds, asked, "haven't we suffered enough from this religion?"

A thirty-four-year-old postal worker argued that he had already started to question the role of religion in his life before the rise of the AKP, primarily due to the injustices against his fellow Kurds. Responding to Turkey's stance toward Kurdish militias in their efforts to defend the border city of Kobani from the Islamic State forces in late 2014, he concluded "I have lost faith in religion." Eccarius-Kelly (2016) draws attention to the significance of the Kurdish struggle and later victory in the Syrian Kurdish town of Kobani. The "Kobani factor," she argues, played a key role in generating long-sought recognition abroad for the Kurds. Another acute observer describes this battle as "a defining moment of nationhood and identity" (Barkey 2014). This interviewee forcefully argued that the battle "made it clear that Turks and Arabs, two Sunni-Muslim majority peoples, do not consider us, the Kurds, as equals but instead a people that they want to subjugate."

The armed conflict has weakened the role religion plays in Kurdish identity and generated negative views and attitudes toward religion. Even practicing Muslim Kurds have experienced an important change in their interpretation of religion as the glue that binds Muslims together. A sixty-two-year-old woman's reaction to then prime minister Ahmet Davutoglu's statement in Diyarbakir, the largest Kurdish-dominated province in the southeast, following the Eid al-Adha prayer on September 24, 2015, attests to this. In his speech Davutoglu emphasized a common [Islamic] past and called for solidarity in the fight against the PKK. He also called for a strong Turkey for all "oppressed" Muslims across the world.[7] The interviewee, herself a devout Muslim whose grandson was fighting in the ranks of the PKK, was furious at the prime minister's reference to "sufferings" in Damascus, Baghdad, Arakan [Myanmar], Somalia, and Palestine while ignoring the Kurdish suffering at the hands of the Turkish state. "Don't you have any shame," she reacted, "to come to my city and ask for solidarity with our Muslim brethren in Somalia and Palestine."

Similar to the views expressed about gender equality in chapter 3, the interviewees who were well-versed in the PKK's underlying ideology or were involved with the Kurdish political movement held noticeably more secular views than those who experienced violence but did not share the insurgent approach to religion. Those who supported or were more disposed to support the PKK experienced secularization in all aspects of their lives and presented an overall religious decline. Others merely highlighted the dangers of mixing religion and politics and argued that Islam should have no place in the Turkish arsenal against the Kurdish struggle for equal rights. Thus, while war experiences have a widespread effect on religious identity, the response to those experiences is shaped by ideological factors.

Despite difficulties involved in identifying the link between war and secularization, ranging from issues with the multidimensional nature of the term "secularization" to concerns and questions regarding survey data, there is significant evidence to support the secularizing effect of armed conflict on societies. The data from a large survey conducted in conflict-torn Kurdish provinces coupled with qualitative testimonies from dozens of individuals, most of whom are practicing Muslims, furnishes evidence for the hypothesized relationship between ethnic conflict and secularization. The armed conflict has weakened the argument for religion as an inclusive supra-identity that can potentially mend ethnic wounds that have festered. In fact, it has essentially changed the relationship between two ethnic groups who hail from the same faith and has resulted in questioning the value of Islam as a common denominator. The conflict has facilitated the emergence of a newly defined and more secular national identity while contributing to negative attitudes toward religion among the Kurds.

Conclusion

This power of religion has attracted many, including political entrepreneurs who seek to utilize its power to legitimize their cause and mobilize their followers. This politicization of religion is also likely to result in competing interpretations and ultimately to pave the way for secularization. Evidence from quantitative as well as qualitative data presented in this chapter shows that war experiences have facilitated the rise of a secular worldview among members of the Kurdish minority. The fight for equal rights against a government dominated by the Muslim Turks has resulted in a decline in religious practices and values.

To be sure, Islam plays a prominent role in Kurdish peoples' lives. Despite the regional, tribal, and ethnic elements involved, the first major Kurdish rebellion in modern Turkey was in part motivated by the new Turkish elites' aggressive secularizing reforms. The Sheik Said Revolt of 1925 was largely driven by the abolition of the Caliphate, an important symbol that tied Muslims together, in 1924 (Olson 1989a). As Soleimani (2016) notes, the rebellion was prompted by a combination of factors including Turkish policies of centralization, Turkification, and secularization. Had it been successful, however, it would have resulted in a Kurdish Caliphate.[8] Moreover, as noted earlier, a majority of the respondents have stated that they pray regularly and that religion is "very important" in their lives. As some scholars have pointed out, the salient role Islam plays in Kurdish society has pressured the PKK to adopt a conciliatory tone with regard to Islam (Sarigil and Fazlioglu 2013).

Secularization is a complex process and is not necessarily antireligious. Instead, it refers to a transformation that engenders a world in which religion matters less. In other words, "individual religious sensitivity," as Dobbelaere (2007, 139) concludes, "is not a falsification of secularization theory, it confirms it and so does religious bricolage." The PKK movement has carried, or at times dragged, traditional Kurdish society into modernity over the past four decades. During this journey, the PKK as an industry has redefined the role and place of religion in the emerging Kurdish identity.

In the process, Islam has been *Kurdified* and has gained a subsidiary role in Kurds' political and social life (Gurses 2015b).

The three-decades-long armed struggle for greater rights for the Kurds in Turkey has transformed traditional Islamic values predominant among the Kurds and resulted in redefining Islam's role in Kurdishness. Islam is no longer a substitute for Kurdish identity but rather has been subordinated to secular ethnonationalist demands. War experiences along with a secular ideology have created an environment that has given rise to detachment from religious identity and a growing identification with ethnic nationalism. This has led to questioning religion's overarching claim, which has resulted in multiple contending interpretations of the role of religion and has engendered a dramatic decline in religious practices, values, and norms.

PART IV

SIX

War and Peace

Peace in the aftermath of civil war has been the subject of many theoretical and empirical studies. As a 2007 United Nations press release stressed, "roughly half of all countries that emerge from war lapse back into violence within five years."[1] Quinn, Mason, and Gurses (2007, 168) observe that the 108 civil wars listed by the Correlates of War dataset for the period between 1944 and 1997 occurred in just 54 countries. The use of an alternative dataset confirms this conclusion: the 124 wars that Doyle and Sambanis (2000) report took place in 69 states, and only 36 of these nations had one civil war. This makes the authors conclude that "for a certain subset of nations, civil war appears to be a chronic condition."

Significantly, due mainly to the indivisible nature of the issues involved, ethnic conflicts are often characterized as particularly intractable (Licklider 1995; Horowitz 2000; Kaufmann 1996; Sambanis 2001). These conflicts involve combatants mobilized along ethnic lines and tend to be secessionist, thus threatening internationally recognized territorial borders. Furthermore, some have argued that the outbreak of conflict among ethnic groups strengthens the "incompatibility of national identities" (Chapman and Roeder 2007, 679) and "destroy(s) the possibilities for ethnic cooperation" (Kaufmann 1996, 137).

While atrocities of civil war make peaceful coexistence difficult, "impossible, even grotesque," it does happen (Licklider 1995, 681). Studies have shown that ethnic cooperation is more common than conflict (Fearon and Laitin 1996), and peace after ethnic civil war is possible provided the state addresses ethnic grievances (Gurses and Rost 2013).

What are the prospects for a peaceful coexistence between Kurds and the Turkish state? By the same token, what are the obstacles to peace? In this chapter, I provide a summary of approaches and findings from the large literature on civil war and postwar peace building and assess the prospects for a democratic and peaceful coexistence between the warring parties.

It is worth stating that the term "peace" in most existing literature refers to negative peace or simply the absence of violence. This is in part due to the conceptualization of civil war as an armed contest involving a government and a nonstate actor generating a certain number of battle-related fatalities, ranging from twenty-five to one thousand annual deaths, depending on one's choice of civil war dataset.[2] When a formulation places an emphasis on annual casualties as a defining feature of civil war, it creates a definition of peace that is simply the absence of violence.

The negative conceptualization of peace is also driven by its simplicity, allowing for cross-national comparison. While the focus on negative peace is partly driven by the fact that "consensus is more easily obtained" (Galtung 1969, 190), the same formulation might account for the recurring nature of civil war. Confining peace to the absence of violence might preclude our ability to diagnose the root causes that put a nation at risk of war.

In this book, "peace" refers to the absence of "structural violence" involving an asymmetrical association from which exploitation and marginalization of the weaker group arises. Overcoming such an uneven relationship necessitates addressing the conditions that turn one party into the permanent or "institutional" loser. Peace, defined as such, points toward "social justice" or an "egalitarian distribution of power and resources" (Galtung 1969, 185; see also Galtung 1985). In the words of Wallensteen (2015, 6), "peace is not simply a matter of being without a war for a period of time," rather "quality peace means the creation of postwar conditions that make the inhabitants of a society secure in life and dignity now and for the foreseeable future."

What Do We Know about Ethnic Civil War and Peace: A Synopsis

Conflict studies have pointed out a broad range of economic, social, and political factors in exploring war and peace. Several works have investigated the link between greed and grievances and included such factors as level of economic development, unequal distribution of wealth, political exclusion, ethnic and religious polarization, access to natural resources, and state weakness to explain causes of civil war (Goodwin and Skocpol 1989;

Elbadawi and Sambanis 2000; Collier and Hoeffler 2004; Humphreys 2005; Hegre and Sambanis 2006; Ross 2006; Gurses and Mason 2010). Despite such a large body of literature and diverse findings, existing approaches to civil war in general and ethnic civil war in particular can be summarized by capacity and willingness to rebel. These two dimensions are often intertwined rather than isolated from one another. An increase in the capacity to rebel may not necessarily lead to an armed confrontation unless it meets with the willingness to engage in a war with the government.

Capacity to rebel refers to opportunities that make rebellion feasible, such as the size and distribution of ethnic groups. Geographically concentrated large ethnic groups can more effectively mobilize for collective action and are more likely to rebel. Group size, Posner (2004) argues, greatly shapes the political salience of cultural cleavages and can serve as a viable basis for political mobilization. Weidman (2009) finds that the spatial proximity of group members facilitates collective action and markedly explains whether dissidents can mount an insurgency. Cederman, Wimmer, and Min (2010) point to group size as a factor that adds to mobilization capacity of groups, increasing the chances of a violent confrontation with the government.

Geography, the physical environment in which potential rebels operate, constitutes another important facet of capacity to rebel. Rough landscapes such as mountains, jungles, and swamps raise the risk of rebellion because they can serve as shelter for the rebels in their fight against the state. Rough terrain also strains the policing capacity of the state and makes it easier for rebels to establish safe areas from which to operate (Fearon and Laitin 2003; Collier and Hoeffler 2004; Buhaug, Cederman, and Rød 2008). In the words of James Kiras (2013, 178), a scholar of counterinsurgency and irregular warfare, "formidable terrain that limits the manoeuvre of government forces" helps offset the rebels' "relative weaknesses in technology, organization, and numbers."

In addition to these domestic factors, a growing number of studies have highlighted the role that transborder networks and connections play in the decision to go to war. As one scholar observes, civil war should not be treated as "a fully domestic phenomenon" as "actors, resources, and events span national boundaries" (Gleditsch 2007, 293–94). The transnational dimensions of civil war are particularly pertinent to ethnic rebellions, as the majority of ethnic groups who have engaged in violent action since World War II have been spread across formal territorial boundaries (Gurses 2015a). Ethnic ties that transcend internationally recognized borders contribute to the capacity to rebel in that these networks offer external sanctuaries, help recruit new members, and gather intelligence from among their ethnic kin in adjacent countries (Saideman and Ayres 2000; Salehyan 2007; Cederman et al. 2013).

Willingness to rebel refers to what others have called the motive and incentives to engage in violent protest. Literature on civil war often cites a sense of deprivation and injustice as the motive for violent action. Earlier works have pointed to the unequal distribution of wealth and political power as the culprit behind violent conflict (Gurr 1993; Horowitz 2000). Building on these grievance-based arguments, a number of recent studies have stated that state policies that systematically restrict ethnic minorities' access to political and economic power play a key role in the decision to resort to violence and prospects for peace in the aftermath of ethnic civil wars (Buhaug, Cederman, and Rød 2008; Wimmer, Cederman, and Min 2009; Cederman, Wimmer, and Min 2010; Gurses and Rost 2013).

As I discuss in greater depth below, factors that increase both the capacity and willingness to rebel are strongly present in the Kurdish case. Group, state, and regime characteristics along with international factors that facilitate group mobilization for political action critically contribute to Kurds' capacity and willingness to rebel.

Obstacles to Peace with the Kurds

Waves of nationalism and increasing saliency of ethnicity in the nineteenth and early twentieth centuries contributed to the collapse of the multinational Ottoman Empire and ushered in a new epoch for modern Turkey that came into existence in 1923. The collapse of the empire after a decade of wars (the Balkan Wars of 1912–13, World War I, and the Turco-Greek war of 1919–22) brought about important demographic changes. The loss of Balkan territories produced a wave of Muslim refugees headed to the Anatolian peninsula that would form the geography of the new Turkey as well as the demise of a large Christian population in the same region. Forced migrations coupled with the mass killings of Armenians (and Assyrians, another non-Muslim community) during World War I resulted in the near extinction of these communities in Anatolia.[3] The "population exchange" agreement signed in 1923 between the governments of Greece and Turkey rid Anatolia of its last large Christian community. As a result of this compulsory exchange, Turkish and Greek governments purged most of the Greek and Muslim/Turkic elements in their societies (Gocek 1996; Hirschon 2003; Clark 2006).

By the time the new Turkish state consolidated its power in the 1930s, Turkey's population consisted primarily of Muslims that included a number of non-Turkic groups such as Kurds, Arabs, Georgians, Bosnians, Macedonians, and Circassians. Of these non-Turkic peoples, Kurds possessed a high capacity to rebel for a number of reasons. First, unlike many of these groups, Kurds were not immigrants or refugees who fled from war as the empire disintegrated. They were indigenous to their lands with a long history of autonomous rule under the Ottomans.

Second, other ethnic minorities were much smaller and spread across the country. This factor facilitated their assimilation into the newly forged Turkish national identity. Kurds, with a population that was at least 10 percent of the total population, were geographically concentrated and formed majorities in the mountainous and underdeveloped regions of southeast and eastern Turkey. According to the 1935 census, Turkish, the official language of Turkey, was spoken by 86 percent of the population (13,899,073 out of a total population of 16,157,450), while Kurdish was spoken by nearly 10 percent of the population. Arabic speakers, the third largest ethnic group at the time the census was held, made up roughly 1 percent (153,687) of the total population (Cagaptay 2004, 93; Koc, Hancioglu, and Cavlin 2008). It should be noted that the actual size of the Kurdish community is likely to be higher considering the political environment in which the census was held along with the state ban on the Kurdish language (Jwaideh 2006, 9–10).

Additionally, despite massive migration movements out of the Kurdish homeland, a large majority (69 percent) of Kurds still live in the eastern regions of Turkey bordering Iraq, Iran, and Syria (Koc, Hancioglu, and Cavlin 2008). In line with studies that have pointed to rugged terrain as a facilitator of war, Kurdish homeland consists of "impassable" (Jwaideh 2006) or "forbidding" (Bruinessen 1992) mountains that have historically served as shelter and haven against foreign invaders.

A third factor that contributes heavily to Kurds' capacity to rebel is their cross-border spread into neighboring Iraq, Iran, and Syria. Jwaideh (2006, 143), in his examination of the Kurds in Syria after World War I, aptly summarizes the interconnectedness of the Kurds and the Kurdish question. The newly drawn borders "did not mean much" for the Kurdish tribesmen in northern Syria as these frontiers "in many cases placed members of the same tribe under two different administrations, French and Turkish." Thus, he concludes that nationalist activities in Syria have been "an echo and extension of Kurdish nationalist activity in Turkey." Recent developments in Syria, Iraq, Turkey, and Iran have only confirmed the regional dimension of the Kurdish question.

The size of their population, geographic concentration, history of autonomy, and transborder linkages—factors one prominent conflict scholar (Gurr 1993, 167) deems as key predictors of political action—added greatly to the Kurdish capacity to challenge the Turkish state. The same factors presented the most formidable test of ethnic homogenization and assimilation policies of the nascent Turkish state. As the single most important obstacle in the path to state and nation building, Kurds came to represent a genuine threat to the very definition of Turkish national identity envisioned by the new Republican elites.

The fate of a Turkish national identity largely hinged on the suppression of Kurdish nationalism. This nonconsensual, coercive, ethnic boundary expansion pursued by the founding elites (Wimmer 2013) sheds considerable light on the antagonistic relationship Kurds have with modern Turkey. This situation, as one observer has pointed out, boils the Kurdish problem in general and the war between Turkey and the PKK in particular down to "a conflict over what it means to be a citizen of Turkey" (Cook 2016). Thus, "incompatible identities" (Chapman and Roeder 2007) or a historical, "genetic disjuncture located at the very *origins* of [modern Turkey]," characterized by a monolingual nation-building model (Akturk 2015, 803), greatly explain the root causes of the Kurdish problem and account for enduring exclusionary state policies toward the Kurds that feed the willingness to rebel.

Incentives for War

Although the Kurds were central to the founding of the country, as they overwhelmingly rallied behind the new Turkish elites fending off Greek, British, French, and Italian invaders in what is often referred to by Turks as the "War of Independence," upon the creation of the new state, promises of autonomy for the Kurds were quickly forgotten (Yegen 2007; Hur 2010). Turkey's ruling elites under Mustafa Kemal's leadership, intent on forging a new national identity centered around Turkish nationalism, embarked on radical social reforms. This rigid formation of national identity based in part on linguistic homogeneity came at the expense of Kurds as the single largest non-Turkic people in the country. Assimilationist policies and rabidly anti-Kurdish state practices aimed at suppressing Kurdish identity and culture included the outright denial of Kurds as a separate nationality, criminalizing the Kurdish language, and a migration policy aimed at diluting the Kurdish-populated provinces (Olson 1989a; Yegen 1996; McDowall 2004; Gunter 2004; Romano 2006, Aslan 2007; Bayir 2013).

As one keen observer of Kurdish studies notes, such an approach turned Kurdish ethnicity and language into targets of sovereign power, making their suppression "necessary to secure sovereign domination and ensure the discursive unity of sovereign identity" (Vali 2016, 290). Turkish national identity defined as such would form the foundation of future conflict between Kurds and the new Turkish state. Although the Turkification policy consisted of social, economic, and cultural aspects (Bayir 2013), nothing shows the extent and severity of this program better than state practices toward the Kurdish language. As part of the campaign to eradicate Kurdish identity, the state renamed Kurdish villages. As McDowall (2004, 427) reports, "by 1986, 2,842 out of 3,524 villages in the Kurdish-majority Adiyaman, Gaziantep, Urfa, Mardin, Siirt, and Diyarbakir had been renamed to expunge Kurdish identity."

Language is of significant value for two main reasons. First, it was (and still is) a key ethnic marker that distinguishes Kurds from the majority Turks despite assimilationist policies. Second, speaking a language that is entirely different from the state's only official language has impeded millions of Kurds from accessing jobs, education, and mainstream politics. Laitin and Ramachandran (2016), building on data from eleven African countries that adopted English as the medium of instruction in the postcolonial era, examine how the choice of official language as a gatekeeper for accessing economic and political opportunities affects the socioeconomic development. They find that the individual's increasing distance from and lower exposure to the official language increases learning cost and, as a result, reduces the level of human capital. Language serves as a barrier to equal opportunity, advantaging those fluent in the language.[4]

Similar to these former colonies in which the adopted official language was spoken by only an elite minority, a vast majority of the Kurds could not speak Turkish during the formative years of the republic. Even today, after nearly a century of state ban on the Kurdish language, many in the countryside cannot speak the official language. The denial of Kurdish has added to the unequal relationship Kurds have with the state by reinforcing the uneven access Kurds have to economic and political resources in Turkey.

The discrimination Kurds face in Turkey is not merely lingual. Tezcur and Gurses (2017) examine Kurdish access to state power since the early years of modern Turkey and demonstrate that the problem is rampant. Kurdish exclusion has proven to be an important aspect of the system and has not varied across time and political ideology. The Kurdish minority's unequal relationship with the state since the foundation of the republic in 1923 was not altered after the transition to multiparty democracy in the 1950s, to a market economy in the 1980s, and after the rise of the Islamist AKP to power in 2002. In fact, religious, class, and ideological differences or rivalries within the majority Turks are often subordinated to common opposition to the Kurds.

The omission of the pro-Kurdish Peoples' Democratic Party (HDP) from the "Rally for Democracy" on August 7, 2016, to denounce that year's coup attempt is a further testament to overall Turkish state policy toward Kurds. Despite the theme of the rally (unity and democracy) a party that stood against the attempted putsch and received more than five million votes was not invited on the grounds that it was no different from the alleged coup plotters,[5] even though the HDP, through its young and eloquent cochair Selahattin Demirtas, effectively appealed to Turkish conscience to find a political solution to the Kurdish question.

Time and again, from one demonstration to another, the HDP publicly condemned separatist views or goals. Despite some internal opposition, Turkeyfication (*Turkiyelilesme*), with an emphasis on finding a democratic solution within Turkey's internationally recognized territorial boundaries, came to occupy center stage. The HDP became the champion for a democratic coexistence, disavowing partitioning of the country. Alas, the government dragged its feet and failed to offer any meaningful change to the Kurdish-state relationship. The door seems to be closed to the Kurds regardless of their tactics or approaches to politics. To apply a soccer metaphor, as soccer enthusiast Turkish president Tayyip Erdogan regularly does, existing state structure has relegated Kurds to the sidelines.

Turkish Social Prejudices

Anti-Kurdishness is not limited to official state policies. Peace and reconciliation require recognition, the extension of dignity and esteem to the "other" through understanding, trust, and respect (Gibson 2004). It also calls for the promotion of empathy to repair social and familial networks damaged or destroyed during the war (Halpern and Weinstein 2004). Turkish social fabric presents itself as an obstacle to such an outcome. A constant stream of derogatory, pejorative labels for the Kurds seems to have become ingrained in Turkish sociopolitical culture. Due in part to the nation-building efforts of the early years that positioned Kurdishness as the "other," anti-Kurdish views and attitudes have become integral to Turkish culture.[6] These attitudes feed the thinly concealed institutional bias against the Kurds and function as an obstacle to a dignified peace.[7]

Celik (2005, 142) notes that Kurdish migrants in Istanbul face "discriminatory, racist practices" in renting apartments and interacting with their Turkish neighbors. "When they had problems with their Turkish neighbors over any issue," some reported that "their neighbors used the word 'Kurd' as a pejorative label." Celik concludes that this practice, which has its roots in a time period that saw an influx of Kurds uprooted because of the conflict, continues today in that Kurds are often treated as "potential criminals."

A recent study by Ulug and Cohrs (2017) explores representations of the Kurdish conflict among laypeople in the multiethnic city of Mersin in southern Turkey. The authors recruit fifteen Turks, fifteen Kurds, and fifteen Arabs through snowball sampling and analyze the data using Q-methodology to uncover socially shared viewpoints. Their detailed analysis of the qualitative data collected from the participants points out five distinct viewpoints. The first and third viewpoints were held by one Kurd each and the second viewpoint by no Kurds. Adherents to the fourth viewpoint included two Kurds, and the fifth viewpoint was held exclusively by Kurds.

The first two viewpoints depict the Kurdish conflict largely in terms of "security" and "economic" perspectives. They strongly oppose the inclusion of the jailed PKK leader, Ocalan, into the peace process and find the implementation of certain constitutional changes that would allow for some form of self-rule for the Kurds "unacceptable." Participants who shared the third viewpoint, while describing the conflict as a result of state authoritarianism or Turkish people's ignorance of the problem, echoed viewpoints 1 and 2 and reject the inclusion of Ocalan into the solution and granting political and social rights to the Kurds. While acknowledging state authoritarianism, these participants were unwilling or unable to overcome their prejudices.

The fourth viewpoint, which was held by two Turks, two Kurds, and one Arab, highlights the denial and suppression of Kurds as important causes of the conflict and offers "a new constitution involving civic and democratic laws that guarantee all ethnic diversities" as an effective solution to the conflict. While it differs from viewpoint 3 in blaming the Turkish state for the conflict and supporting more rights to the Kurds, changing the official language of Turkey is rejected. The fifth viewpoint, which was held only by Kurds, draws attention to "long-term denial, suppression, and humiliation of Kurds" as the causes of the conflict. It offers the inclusion of the PKK leader into the peace process, underlines the Kurdish right to autonomy, and acknowledges the need for multiple official languages.

It should be noted that the "pro-Turkish" viewpoints (1 and 2) parallel official views in rejecting the lack of political representation of the Kurds. This perspective emphasizes "outside influence" and "economic problems" as the causes of the conflict. As a result it strongly rejects the inclusion of Ocalan into the solution process and opposes granting political and cultural rights to the Kurds. Instead, reducing unemployment and the PKK laying down its weapons are seen as effective solutions. Moreover, this viewpoint perceives Kurds as "ignorant" and as "separatists" aiming to undermine Turkish territorial unity.

Kose and Yilmaz (2012, 911–14), drew on Billig's (1995) banal nationalism to examine embedded messages to "explore the banalized use of routinely formed nationalist assumptions and positions" in Turkey. Banal nationalism is often unnoticed yet reproduced on a daily basis as it penetrates daily life and routines. Their extensive analysis of 3,146 news items and 462 columns in thirty-six newspapers published on February 3, 2010, shows that Turkish news dailies irrespective of their ideological affiliation "whisper nationalism on an ordinary day." They find that even on a usual day where no development occurred that would call for flagging nationalism, such words as Turk and Turkishness were heavily used in the news items and columns. Moreover, in a further testament to the daily reproduction of Turkish nationalism, 81 percent of the newspapers used the colors red and white (the colors of the Turkish flag) and more than one-third of these newspapers used such slogans as "Turkey belongs to the Turks" or "How happy is he who can say I am a Turk" in their logos.

Somer (2010, 568, 572), building on a systematic content analysis of the main religious and secular newspapers between 1996 and 2004 in Turkey, reaches the conclusion that there is no significant difference between the secular and religious press in their views of the Kurdish question despite signs of a "significant convergence on the overall value of political democracy between the religious and secular press." In other words, although "religious and secular press gave almost equal weight to electoral democracy, liberal democracy, modernization, and social pluralism," when it comes to "suspicion of Kurdish nationalism" or support for a Kurdish opening that would include such concrete reforms as education in Kurdish language, both the religious and secular press were equally resistant to a substantial change in the treatment of the Kurds in Turkey.

In his critique of the myth that science is objective criteria, *The Mismea-*

sure of Man, Stephen Jay Gould argues that science is a socially embedded activity because it must be done by people. Only when scientists can discard the constraints of their culture can one speak of objectivity (1981, 21). Gould (1981, 74) draws attention to how the "apostles of objectivity" used "science" to illustrate a priori conclusions.

Vamik Volkan's views on the Kurdish issue and his stance toward the PKK and its leader shed light on hidden, unconscious aspects of anti-Kurdishness. In *Bloodlines*, Volkan, a renowned Turkish American psychoanalyst, explores ethnic violence through a psychoanalytic lens using evidence from such cases as the Arab/Palestinian–Israeli conflict, the long-running rivalry between Turkey and Greece, the bloody disintegration of the former Yugoslavia, and ethnic tensions between the Baltic countries that gained their independence after the collapse of the Soviet Union and Russia as the successor of the Soviet empire.

When examining the Kurdish conflict in Turkey, which receives only a superficial treatment, Volkan builds his case on a single source written by a journalist with questionable background and credibility. The language and tone used in analyzing this case differ significantly than the type of analytical framework used in examining other conflicts. For example, explaining the civil war and ensuing genocide in Rwanda in the 1990s, the author (12–15) aptly points out the colonial legacy that laid the groundwork for subsequent uneven ethnic relations between Tutsi and Hutu. Similarly, he highlights the significance of the Soviet subjugation, humiliation, and "systematic program of enforced Russification" (139) to examine the root causes of ethnic tensions in Latvia in the 1990s.

His examination of the PKK conflict, however, includes many unsubstantiated claims. The author conveniently dismisses a plethora of studies that have highlighted aggressive assimilationist state policies and practices toward the Kurds. While "enforced Russification," according to the author, accounts for the conflict between Latvia and Russia, Volkan argues that "Turkish Kurds could (and still can) be found in all parts of the country and in all professions" (169), and glosses over enforced Turkification directed at eliminating Kurdishness in Turkey. In the words of Sirri Sureyya Onder, a prominent member of the Kurdish HDP and an ethnic Turk, Kurds can only occupy important positions in Turkey when they are willing to forgo their ethnic identity (Tezcur and Gurses 2017). Volkan's overall perspective appears to be in line with the official view and is more ideologically than scientifically driven. That is, in the words of Gould (1981, 80), "prior prejudice, not copious numerical documentation" seems to dictate his analysis and conclusions.[8]

Responses to Negative Stimuli

On the Kurdish front, two main factors are increasingly weakening the prospects for a peaceful and democratic coexistence. The first relates to the dramatic changes that three decades of armed conflict have brought about in the social fabric of the country. While the Kurdish region has endured most of the burden, the conflict has impacted the entire country at multiple levels. It has been a detriment to Turkey's economy,[9] tarnished its image in the international arena, and created a rift between the Turks and the Kurdish minority. As Yegen (2007) observes, despite the initial goal of aggressive and wide-ranging assimilationist state policies aimed at Turkifying Kurds and treating them as future or potential Turks, over time the Turkish political elites have begun to give up on the hopes that Kurds can be successfully assimilated into the Turkish national identity.[10] In further support of this argument, Kibris (2011) shows that the armed conflict has resulted in "less concessionist" attitudes among ordinary Turks, leading to an increase in the vote share of right-wing Turkish parties with more uncompromising positions on the issue.

Furthermore, while the Kurds by and large are willing to support a peaceful and democratic coexistence with the majority Turks (Kibris 2011), the conflict has begun to erode their hopes for living together in harmony. Results from two nationwide surveys conducted in 2011 and 2013 show that despite relatively higher support for autonomy among the Kurds, support for secession has increased from 23.3 percent to 32.1 percent in two years (Sarigil and Karakoc 2016). The continuation of unequal treatment of the Kurds coupled with dramatic changes taking place in Turkey and neighboring Syria and Iraq, which have largely worked in favor of Kurds in these countries, are likely to feed their desire for secession.

The transborder spread of the Kurds constitutes another important aspect in the war and peace debate. Developments across Turkey's southern border that resulted in significant gains and recognition for the Kurds in Syria have been portrayed by the Turkish government as such a threat to its national security that a progovernment Turkish newspaper warned its readers that the Kurdish PYD of Syria is more dangerous than the IS (Calislar 2015). This portrayal coupled with fear of Kurdish gains in Syria greatly accounts for the overall Turkish foreign policy in that conflict. During the months-long siege of Kobani, the Syrian Kurdish town across from Turkey's southern border, the Turkish army prevented many Kurds in Turkey from crossing the border to help defend the city against the Islamic State's onslaught. In a gleeful speech to an audience consisting of Arab refugees near the Turkish-Syrian border, President Erdogan "discounted" the Kurdish fight against IS and stated that "Kobani is about to fall." This, coupled with the long insurgency in Turkey, resulted in anger, frustration, and dismay among many Kurds. Antigovernment anger boiled over shortly after President Erdogan's comments, resulting in week-long widespread protests in the Kurdish southeast during which at least fifty people lost their lives.[11]

Kurdish restiveness gave in to estrangement after the Battle of Kobani. The actions of the AKP government, which had long invoked Islamic brotherhood as an all-inclusive platform to win over the Kurds, goaded many previously conservative Muslim Kurds to the secular Kurdish HDP. In many ways this frustration helped the secular HDP make inroads among socially conservative Kurds who had long supported the AKP or center-right political parties. Disillusionment with so-called "Islam as a common denominator" and the overall Turkish approach to Kurdish gains in Syria led, in the words of Sirri Sakik (a veteran Kurdish politician and mayor of Kurdish town of Agri), to a "revolt of consciousness" and contributed to many Kurds abandoning the AKP in June 2015 elections (Kasapoglu 2015). The fragile peace process came to an end soon after, dashing the hopes for a peaceful coexistence between the two peoples.

Conclusion

Kurdish ascendance as a domestic political player, coupled with the emergence of the Kurdish PYD in Syria as the United States's most effective partner, played key roles in the collapse of the ceasefire between the Turkish government and the PKK in 2015. Intensification of the armed conflict since July 2015, with the Turkish army laying siege to several Kurdish cities and towns, has produced thousands of casualties and widespread destruction of buildings and property in the Kurdish southeast.

After about six months, thousands of troops, and unprecedented physical destruction, an estimated one thousand PKK militants and militias were dislodged from a number of cities in the Kurdish east. Parts of the ancient Sur district of the Kurdish province of Diyarbakir were literally razed to the ground by the Turkish army to regain control from Kurdish insurgents. By the time the army announced an end to its "cleanup" operations, these cities (notably, the Sur district of Diyarbakir, Cizre, Sirnak, and Silopi) were nearly uninhabitable to the nearly 500,000 civilians forced out by the conflict.

Recent confrontations have shown that the Turkish state is capable in fending off the military threat posed by the PKK. Thus an argument can be made for a Turkish victory in a purely military sense, as it eventually dislodged the PKK from the urban areas. Nonetheless, the most immediate impact of this phase of the three-decades-long armed conflict has been a loss of legitimacy among the vast majority of the Kurds.

While the concept of legitimacy is multidimensional, it is closely tied to the perception of the involved parties or whether the dominated perceive the dominance as rightful (Weber 1946). It refers to the link that ties the population to a state, or the presence of agreement on "what constitutes polity—the politically defined community that underlies the state" (Englebert 2000, 8). Anderson (1987, 2), in her examination of statehood in the Middle East and North Africa, points out that weak states, similar to a "weak" ego, are characterized by aggressive or defensive behavior. Strong states, just like a "strong" ego, accommodate popular demands while weak states often resort to violence and suppression. Thus, as Anderson concludes, "a state which successfully monopolizes the legitimate use of force does so as much because of popular acquiescence as of naked power."

The current situation, despite Turkish military might, is increasingly resembling what Tilly (1978, 200) calls the condition of *dual sovereignty*, characterized by the emergence of contenders who enjoy support from a significant segment of the population and lay exclusive alternative claims to control over the government. Such a situation, along with the inability or unwillingness of the government to suppress the challenge, makes civil war necessary and feasible. As the state presence in the Kurdish regions is increasingly reduced to armored vehicles, military helicopters, and the sounds of warplanes, Turkey-Kurdish relations are devolving into a phase with a colonial ambiance.

The messages left behind by Turkish security forces in the forms of graffiti after the "cleanup" operations, such as "you will see the power of Turk" and "be proud if you are a Turk, obey if you are not," attest to the gravity of the situation (Sabanci 2015). In line with Horowitz's (2000, 7) observation that "in deeply divided societies, strong ethnic allegiances permeate organizations, activities, and roles to which they are formally unrelated," the third-tier football club Diyarbakir's Amedspor midfielder Deniz Naki was banned for twelve games by the Turkish Football Federation for "ideological propaganda" after using social media to dedicate their win against the top-tier Bursaspor to the Kurds killed in Sur and Cizre (Sharma 2016).

Despite atrocities of war and difficulties involved in ethnic civil wars, cooperation and peaceful coexistence is possible. Having the capacity to rebel does not and should not necessarily lead to bloody civil wars. Achieving a sustainable peace in the positive sense, however, will require more than cosmetic solutions to the institutional bias against the Kurds. Since Kurdish capacity for rebellion (as more than two dozen armed insurrections since the 1920s attest[12]) is unlikely to change, the road to peace first and foremost needs to be paved with constitutional reforms targeted to reduce willingness or motives for violent action.

No time period provided a better opportunity than the early 2000s for introducing reforms to reduce Kurdish willingness to rebel and offer a peaceful solution to the PKK-led Kurdish insurrection. Following the PKK leader's capture in 1999, the insurgent group announced a unilateral ceasefire and withdrew from Turkish soil. At its 8th Congress in 2002, while refusing to dismantle its armed wing, the PKK nonetheless changed its name to the Kurdistan Freedom and Democracy Congress (KADEK) and announced its commitment to nonviolent means in its struggle for Kurdish rights. These changes accompanied the rise of the AKP to power and the AKP's successive electoral successes and seemingly softer approach to Kurdish demands. This period hence offered what two keen observers of Turkish politics call a "critical turning point," "periods of broad societal change often involving the institutionalization of new political arrangements" that could have changed the course of the conflict (Barkey and Fuller 1997, 59).

The AKP, claiming to be the voice of largely excluded conservative Muslim masses, championed human rights and democracy. The social and political reforms introduced by the AKP in the early 2000s brought Turkey closer to European Union membership as evidenced by its becoming an official candidate state for membership in 2005. Within this framework, the AKP government introduced a number of reform packages to address the restive Kurdish minority demands. Between 2009 and 2012, measures labeled as "Kurdish Initiative," then changed to "Democratic Opening," and, finally, pointing out that the package does not exclusively deal with the Kurdish demands, diluted to "Unity and Brotherhood Project." These policies resulted in changes that included a twenty-four-hour Kurdish language TV station, a two-year master's degree program on Kurdish language and culture, and allowing Kurdish language to be offered as an elective course at the fifth-grade level (Gurses 2010, 2014; Somer and Liaras 2010).

Although this period saw some deviations from the dominant narrative of the Turkish state that treats the PKK as the cause, not the symptom, of Turkish-Kurdish conflicts, "these deviations did not develop into a coherent and consistent alternative narrative" (Rumelili and Celik 2017, 8). The so-called Unity and Brotherhood Project forcefully argued for keeping the state's unitary structure intact, vowed to preserve its only official language, and called for "one state, one nation, one homeland, one flag."[13]

Thus, as Somer (2010, 573) notes, although the AKP might have felt compelled to launch reforms to address the Kurdish conflict through negotiations and democratic political reforms, the Islamist elites by and large do not differ in their views of the Kurdish problem than the secular elites. While Turkish Islamists had long ascribed the root causes of the Kurdish question to the previous secularist state structure, they seem to lack sufficient ideological preparation to fully implement reforms aimed at restructuring the state to be inclusive of Kurds. Instead, since their ascent to power—rather than democratizing the state, which could have provided a real platform to democratically address the grievances of both the previously excluded Muslim groups as well as the Kurdish minority—they appear to have been preoccupied with consolidating their power (Somer 2016, 2). In other words, the Islamist movement in Turkey "bears the fingerprints of nationalistic discourse," which makes it "unable to find a position properly sensitive of Kurdish suffering" (Houston 2001, 141–42; also see Cicek 2011).

Similar to earlier critical points (such as the early years of the republic during which a more relaxed version of Turkish national identity could have been devised to avoid the rise of Kurdish nationalism, or the transition to multiparty rule in the 1950s, which could have been used to address Kurdish demands democratically), this opportunity too was missed due mainly to "the state's unwillingness to confront the Kurdish question in other than a primarily military dimension" (Barkey and Fuller 1997, 78).

Rather than tackling the underlying Kurdish unequal relationship with the system, the "opening" merely eased restrictions on the expression of Kurdish cultural identity and failed to make a dent in deep-seated grievances. Lacking constitutional guarantees, these half-hearted reforms are at the government's mercy and can be reversed at any time. Importantly, the words "Kurd" or "Kurdish" have been carefully avoided in all official documents. Instead, Kurdish is referred to as "other languages" or lumped into the so-called "living languages" as a way of dismissing it or reducing it to an exotic creature in need of state "protection," rather than the language of the second largest ethnic group in the country.

While symbolic and cosmetic in nature, the "opening" represented a moment of hope. The crackdown on the Kurdish movement since the collapse of the ceasefire in mid-2015, along with Turkey's continuing drift to authoritarianism, however, has effectively annulled these reforms. In

September 2016, the AKP government removed two dozen democratically elected Kurdish mayors and appointed governors as trustees in their stead. By January 2017, the number of democratically elected mayors replaced by the government reached fifty-four, including mayors of the three metropolitan municipalities of Diyarbakir, Van, and Mardin. The elected comayor of Mardin, Ahmet Turk, a seventy-four-year-old veteran Kurdish politician, was dismissed from his duty on "terror" charges and later arrested. The cochairman of the HDP, Demirtas, was arrested in the Kurdish city of Diyarbakir in the southeast but sent to a high-security prison in Edirne, a western province bordering Bulgaria and Greece. The comayor of Mardin was transferred to Istanbul's Silivri Prison, nearly a thousand miles away from his hometown.[14]

In early January 2017, the trustee who was appointed to the Kayapinar Municipality in Diyarbakir ordered the destruction of a monument constructed to commemorate the 2011 death of thirty-four Kurdish civilians, mostly young boys, in the village of Roboski (Uludere) by Turkish Air Force jets.[15] The Kurdish Institute of Istanbul, a nongovernmental organization founded in the 1990s to preserve Kurdish language and literature, was closed down as part of the suppression of the Kurdish movement. This closure, in the words of the institute's cochair, represents a return to the original position of the Turkish state when Kurdish existence was denied and repressed (M. Bozarslan 2017).

Given a high capacity for rebellion and the systematic exclusionary state policies toward the Kurds that are ingrained in the origins of the republic, reforms aimed at relaxing restrictions on Kurdishness without addressing the fundamentals of the state are unlikely to address this antagonistic relationship. Since "birth legacy" is found to be a significant predictor of capabilities, regime type, and political stability (Lemke and Carter 2016), without a change in the republic's national identity (what it means to be a citizen of Turkey) positive peace is an unlikely outcome. In fact, given the Kurdish capacity for rebellion that is further augmented by the changes in neighboring Syria and Iraq, even a negative peace is unlikely to be achieved.

Making and keeping peace is arguably more complex and challenging than war. This is particularly true after the onset of armed conflict that pits one ethnic group against another. War dynamics destroy trust and weaken the desirability of coexistence, making peace in the positive sense hard to achieve. Peace building, as Goldberg (2016) argues at length, is a complex phenomenon and thus requires a comprehensive approach to resolve the conflict issues. It vigorously requires more than agreeing to a ceasefire or even a peace agreement signed by the antagonists. It also calls for overcoming anger, fear, and distrust between the warring groups.

Thus, peace between the Kurds and the Turkish state will require reforms at social, cultural, economic, and political levels. As Jacoby and Ozerdem aptly summarize (2013, 125), the change at the state level alone will not be sufficient for a successful conflict transformation in Turkey. The disarmament of the PKK should accompany the "demilitarization of minds" to allow for the Kurds to live in dignity and harmony with majority Turks. Socially, as outlined earlier, anti-Kurdish views and attitudes need to change. Culturally, the Kurdish language should be treated as the language of the second largest group in the country rather than a historical artifact in need of state protection. Economically, policies and measures to lift the Kurdish region out of poverty could facilitate peace. Most importantly, there is a need to redefine Turkish national identity to one with which Kurds can identify. Without such a drastic and comprehensive approach to the Kurdish question, halfhearted measures aimed at avoiding the problem will fail. Absent reforms on multiple levels to gain the hearts and minds of the aggrieved Kurds, any "opening" is likely to be dismissed by the Kurds as a public relations gimmick or a ploy to save time.

Critics of the partition argument have pointed to the difficulties and unrealistic assumptions of creating defensible ethnic enclaves (Sambanis 2000; Sambanis and Schulhofer-Wohl 2009), stressed that partition may not necessarily resolve the root causes of conflict (Christie 1992; Horowitz 2003), and stated that partition is unlikely to produce ethnically homogenous states (Horowitz 2000). One can, however, marshal equally scholarly evidence for partition reducing the chance of further conflict (Kaufmann 1996; Chapman and Roeder 2007). To be sure, partition as a solution to ethnic civil wars should be the last resort, only to be implemented in particular cases (Horowitz 2000), and the phenomena of separatism "must concentrate on the specific, inherent characteristics of the identity of group" and "the unique circumstances and historical events that helped forged that identity" (Christie 1996, vii). Absent a radical transformation of the Turkish state and national identity, the Kurdish case is approaching a stage where separation of the warring parties might be the best solution for building and sustaining peace.

SEVEN

Conclusion

This study is an attempt to shed light on the complex nature of civil war. It joins the debate on the need to shift the focus from macro-level analyses to the micro-level in examining the complex nature of violent conflict. Drawing on the PKK insurgency in Turkey, I aimed to dissect the multifaceted phenomenon of war by demonstrating that conflict can pave the way for positive sociopolitical changes.

Evidence from the Kurdish conflict both vindicates and challenges current findings outlined in the growing literature on the war-change spectrum. While the results presented in this book confirm previous studies that have drawn attention to armed conflict's potential to engender greater political activism, they have also highlighted the key role ideology plays in providing gains in women's rights and secularization.

As discussed in chapter 4, armed conflict helps articulate social, economic, and political grievances in a society and paves the way for the rise of an activist identity. These results resonate well with previous findings by scholars who have argued for the positive outcomes of conflict (Wood 2003; Bellows and Miguel 2009; Blattman 2009).

The argument and results presented also speak to the literature on civil war and democratization. While most existing studies rely on war characteristics, such as outcome, type, deadliness, and duration, to model post-civil-war democratization (Wantchekon 2004; Gurses and Mason 2008; Joshi 2010; Nilsson 2012), this study demonstrates that wartime experiences also help engender a democratic political culture at the individual level. War dynamics not only facilitate the rise of an activist identity characterized by a willingness to participate but also help build a capacity for empathy. Additionally, it highlights the war–nation-building connection and its effects on creating a sense of belonging, a common consciousness that makes up an important part of political culture. Similar to what Tilly (1975, 1990) argued with regard to how war made states in Europe, civil war dynamics facilitate the rise of an ethnonational identity, or a "national unity" as "the sole background condition" of building and sustaining democracy (Rustow 1970, 350).

Nonetheless, as discussed at length in chapter 2, insurgent groups' ideology is of significant importance in explaining changes in gender relations and religious decline. While ideology is often neglected in civil war studies, it can serve as a blueprint that guides and regulates insurgent groups' behavior (Gutierrez-Sanin and Wood 2014). Ideology helps participants to make sense of their pain and suffering and provide a proper language with which individuals can express their anger, frustration, and desires.

Results presented in chapters 3 and 5 confirm the key role ideology plays in bringing about social change. The hypothesized effects of wartime experiences producing gender-equal attitudes and leading to noticeable secularization are largely conditioned by the insurgent group's ideology. Thus, in line with some recent scholarly works that have highlighted the effects of leftist ideology on encouraging women's participation in armed conflict (Huang 2016; Wood and Thomas 2017), the PKK's ideology has had a noticeable impact on producing an environment conducive to more gender equal relations[1] and resulting in an observable secularization among the Kurds.

Drawing on the estimated proportion of an insurgent group's combat force made up of women, Wood and Thomas (2017) categorize all insurgent groups that were active between 1979 and 2009. Their measure of "female combatant prevalence" ranges from "0" (none/no evidence) to "1" (low, <5 percent), to "2" (moderate, 5 percent–20 percent) and to "3" (high, >20 percent) prevalence. Of the sixteen groups that received a "high" score, an outcome the authors ascribe to a leftist ideology, the PKK is the only major insurgent group from a majority Muslim society.[2]

The emphasis on gender equality often sets insurrections espousing leftist views apart from other groups, Islamists in particular. An Islamist worldview often strives to preserve non-egalitarian gender views that turn "reality into a false (and therefore unchangeable) 'reality'" (Freire 2000, 37). The issue of women, as Talhami (1996, 123) examines at length using the case of Egypt (a country home to the Muslim Brotherhood, arguably the largest and most influential Islamist movement in the world), is the Achilles' heel of Islamism. This issue, Talhami writes, has become "the most objectionable feature of the Islamist blueprint for social change," despite attempts by various Islamists to refute the charge of women's unequal treatment in Islam.

Evidence from post-1979 Iran confirms the significance of ideology in facilitating or obstructing gains in women's rights. The Iranian case resembles the aforementioned cases of Uganda and Rwanda, two cases that experienced significant gains in women's rights, in that the Khomeini-led opposition won a decisive military victory against the shah's regime. In contrast to Uganda and Rwanda, postrevolutionary Iran "encouraged motherhood and domesticity" as women's important duties. The emphasis on Islamic law placed women "in an unequal position with regard to polygyny, divorce, and child custody" (Ramazani 1993, 411).

It was the death of Khomeini and the rise of a reformist government to power in the 1990s that created "a climate more receptive to reform on issues affecting women" (Ramazani 1993, 409). Harsh and extremist measures on women introduced by the revolutionary regime were progressively modified due partly to the "politicization of women during the revolution and the resultant sense of empowerment" (Kazemi 2000, 465). This partial progress, made after the end of the Khomeini era characterized by strict enforcement of veiling and gender segregation, came under severe pressure with the election of Ahmadinejad in 2005. With the ascendency of Ahmadinejad to power, conservative Islamic ideas toward women reappeared in the public discourse as the government "tried to discourage women's public presence by getting them back to their natural role as mothers and nurturers" (Rezai-Rashti 2015, 479).

Thus, while wartime experiences seem to robustly predict greater support for political activism, as demonstrated in chapter 4, changes in attitudes toward women and the rise of a secular political culture appear to be primarily shaped by wartime experiences interacting with insurgent ideology. These findings point to the need to account for the contextual nature of the war-change relationship. They also call for greater scrutiny in analyzing the effects of exposure to violence during civil war on the "remarkable and miraculous" (Guo 2016) sociopolitical changes it produces.

Chapter 6 shifted gear toward the difficult question of peace after ethnic civil wars. It raised questions about the narrow definition of peace used in the extant literature, and it underlined the multifaceted nature of peace building, particularly after ethnic civil wars. Demonstrating the uneven relation between the Kurds and the Turkish state, this chapter casts light on the political, economic, and social obstacles to building a sustainable and dignified peace.

Just as ethnic exclusion is "inimical to democratic principles" (Horowitz 1993, 25), the incorporation of the Kurds into the polity can greatly contribute to deepening and strengthening existing democratic institutions in Turkey. Kurdish inclusion through devolution of power can not only "help avert separatism" (Horowitz 1993, 36), but also build a pluralist democracy that can usher in changes for other smaller, "forgotten" ethnoreligious minorities throughout the region. In a country that once viewed non-Muslim religious minorities as an obstacle to its national unity and security, the Kurdish HDP nominated members of Aramaic-speaking Syriac (Assyrian) Christians and Yezidis, whose ancient religion draws heavily on Zoroastrianism and has become nearly extinct after centuries of oppression. The HDP's Garo Paylan became one of the first Armenians to enter the Turkish parliament (Yackley 2015).

While the Kurdish PYD of Syria has embarked on establishing its own "relatively peaceful and democratic administration" with an emphasis on liberating Kurdish and non-Kurdish women (McKernan 2017), several Kurdish-run municipalities in Turkey introduced measures aimed at reconnecting with the region's multireligious and multiethnic past. In an effort to resuscitate the nearly extinct Armenian and Assyrian cultures in cities where these two Christian communities once held sizeable populations, the Sur municipality of Diyarbakir (a bastion of Kurdish nationalism) helped reconstruct the Surp Giragos Church in 2011. Furthermore, it erected the Monument of Common Conscience in 2013 to raise awareness about the atrocities committed against these communities in the past and to incentivize a democratic coexistence commensurate with Mesopotamia's diverse and rich history. It also began an initiative to offer services in four languages: Turkish, Kurdish, Armenian, and Assyrian.

The Kurdish movement can also strengthen democratic institutions and culture in Turkey through its push for a gender-equal society. The real divide between Western and majority-Muslim countries lies in Western ideological support for equal rights and opportunities for women (Inglehart and Norris 2003). Fish (2002) ascribes the democratic deficit in Muslim societies to the "subordination of women." Moghadam (2004, 3), highlighting the key role the empowerment of women plays in the quality of democracy, concludes that "women may need democracy in order to flourish, but the converse is also true: democracy needs women if it is to be an inclusive, representative, and enduring system of government." The Kurdish HDP has been described as "prowomen" and is credited for reaching out to a variety of minority groups excluded by other parties (Robins-Early 2015).

By the same token, the crackdown on the Kurdish movement carries the risk of undoing the progress made toward gender equality and "threatens a haven of gender equality built by Kurds . . . in a region where patriarchy is generally the rule" (Nordland 2016). Moreover, it is likely to result in reversing the sociopolitical environment that allowed for having a meaningful debate on how to reconcile the region's bloody past. In the aftermath of removing dozens of elected Kurdish mayors, the state-appointed trustee replaced the sign on the Sur municipal building (in the above-mentioned district of Diyarbakir that was written in four languages and emphasized the multireligious and multiethnic past of the city) with a Turkish flag.[3]

The denial of the Kurdish reality or the Turkish state's insistence on the use of military force to deal with Kurdish opposition in Turkey and beyond carries serious risks for further bloodshed and chaos. As Wadie Jwaideh (2006, xvi) prophetically put it in the late 1950s, "the Kurds have come to play an increasingly significant role in Middle Eastern affairs. Their behavior is one of the most important factors in the future stability and security not only of the Kurdish-inhabited countries, but of the entire Middle East." He concludes that "no major country interested in the Middle East can afford to ignore the Kurdish problem or to avoid the formulation of a Kurdish policy as part of its overall Middle Eastern policy" (295).

The sheer size of the Kurds and the lands they inhabit; the division of them between Turkey, Iran, Iraq, and Syria; the collapse of state authorities in Syria and Iraq, which has empowered the Kurdish groups in these countries; and the emergence of Kurds in the Middle East as an effective on-the-ground partner in the fight against Islamic radicalism complicate the Kurdish conflict in Turkey and call for a comprehensive solution to the Kurdish question. As Barkey and Fuller (1997) observe, since the Turkish state has almost always had the initiative, much of the onus of bringing about a sustainable peace is on the Turkish state. In the absence of a real democratic compromise, the situation will most likely result in a weakened state followed by a fractured society and country.

Notes

INTRODUCTION

1. For varying estimates of the size of Kurdish population see Bruinessen (1992, 14–15); Jwaideh (2006, 9–10).

2. "Iran Warns Iraqi Kurdistan against Independence," July 9, 2014, http://en.farsnews.com/newstext.aspx?nn=13930418001290, accessed May 17, 2016.

3. Kurdish lands roughly encompass the area between the northwestern Zagros and the eastern Taurus mountain ranges.

4. It should be noted that due in part to the transborder spread of the large Kurdish population, a number of Kurdish groups have emerged to claim Kurdish leadership. These groups differ in their ideology and goals and compete for power and influence that has resulted in infighting and rivalry. While the PKK is the hegemonic Kurdish organization in Turkey, it is competing with other Kurdish groups in Iran and significantly lags behind the Kurdistan Democratic Party (KDP) and Patriotic Union of Kurdistan (PUK) in northern Iraq. As the subtitle of this book illustrates and as I explain below, my goal is to analyze the conflict-change nexus, using the case of the PKK insurgency in Turkey.

5. The group is also known as ISIS (Islamic State in Iraq and al-Sham), ISIL (Islamic State in Iraq and the Levant), or by its Arabic acronym, DAESH.

6. Ethnic war is defined as wars among communities (ethnicities) that are at odds with the identity of a state and in which ethnic challengers seek to redefine or divide the state itself, or strive for major changes in their relationship with the state (Sambanis 2001, 261–62).

7. It should be noted that the PYD of Syria and the Party of Free Life of Kurdistan in Iran (PJAK) are not simple "mechanical" extensions of the PKK but rather are inspired by the PKK's model and ideology (H. Bozarslan 2017).

Abbas Vali, an expert on Kurdish politics, voices a similar opinion. "Interview with Professor Abbas Vali," *Washington Kurdish Institute*, February 10, 2016, http://dckurd.org/2016/02/24/interview-with-professor-abbas-vali-2/, accessed September 10, 2016.

8. According to a nationwide survey in 2010, the Kurds have an average education of 6.0 years, compared to 8.1 years for the Turks (KONDA 2010).

9. Solati (2017), using ten such proxies, measures patriarchy for forty-nine countries between 1980 and 2011. Her analysis shows that the Middle East and North Africa (including Turkey) is the most patriarchal region of the world.

10. A plethora of studies provide lengthy historical discussions of the Kurdish question. Given the focus of this book, I offer a brief account of the origins and evolution of the PKK.

11. Zeid Ra'ad Al Hussein, the UN high commissioner for human rights, voiced concern about alleged Turkish military abuses, such as allowing more than one hundred people to burn to death while sheltering in basements in the town of Cizre and the deliberate targeting of unarmed civilians, including women and children. http://tribune.com.pk/story/1100523/alleged-turkish-military-abuses-extremely-alarming-un/ May 10, 2016, accessed May 13, 2016.

12. Participants were reminded of their rights and only those who consented were interviewed. No incentive was provided to survey participants.

13. Local teams included female Kurdish interviewers to reduce social desirability bias and increase the response rate among the female participants.

14. The decision to determine the appropriate sample size is a function of precision, confidence, and variability. Yamane (1967, 886) offers the following formula to calculate the sample size: $n = N1+N (e)2$ where n is the sample size, N is the population size, and e is the level of precision. For a large population (i.e., when N>100,000) the appropriate sample size is 400 (a 95 percent confidence level, P = .5, and e = ±5 are assumed). Changing the precision level from e = ±5 to e = ±3 produces a sample size of 1,111 (as reported in Israel, Glenn D. *Determining Sample Size* available at http://edis.ifas.ufl.edu/pdffiles/PD/PD00600.pdf). All three provinces have large populations and are comparable in their population size. Scholte et al. (2004), in their analysis of traumatic events as a result of decades of armed conflict in Afghanistan, assume a prevalence rate of 50 percent. This rate is a safe assumption and can be applied to the case analyzed in this study. The authors estimate that a sample of 770 would be required for a 95 percent confidence interval and a prevalence rate between 45 percent and 55 percent. Therefore, the sample size was set equal to 700 for each province.

15. The overall response rate (52 percent) might seem low but considering difficulties involved in gathering information in environments characterized by large-scale violence (Fujii 2010) and the politically sensitive topic of exposure to violence, this response rate is significant.

16. Different types of exposure to violence are likely to be associated with different outcomes. I return to this issue in detail in the theory section.

17. These results are based on the responses to six individual questions listed in table 2.

18. Although this study is a culmination of several years of data gathering, field trips to multiple countries, and writing, the bulk of the interviews were conducted between December 2013 and August 2016. More specifically, the interviews regarding the effects of the conflict on gender relations (chapter 3) were conducted in December 2013 in Canada (Toronto), the summer of 2014 in Turkey (Diyarbakir, Batman, and Istanbul), and the summer of 2015 in Belgium (Brussels and Antwerp). In the fall of 2015, during which I was on sabbatical leave, I conducted a second round of interviews on the effects of conflict on religion in Turkey. A large majority of this sample (80 percent) was drawn from Diyarbakir, with the remaining coming from Batman, Istanbul, and Mus provinces.

19. For the benefits of using a nonrandom snowball sampling method in qualitative research and conflict environments, see Tansey (2007) and Cohen and Arieli (2011), respectively.

CHAPTER I

1. It is commonly estimated that the conflict had killed around 40,000 people before the outbreak of violence in July 2015 (see, for instance, Tezcur 2014). According to the former chief of staff, Ilker Basbug, between 1984 and 2008 more than 44,000 (32,000 PKK militants, 5,660 civilians, and 6,481 members of Turkish security forces) died as a result of the conflict (Yetkin 2008).

2. "Turkey's PKK Conflict: The Rising Death Tolls," http://www.crisis group.be/interactives/turkey/, accessed May 19, 2017.

3. World Report 2015: Colombia, https://www.hrw.org/world-report/2015/country-chapters/colombia, accessed September 14, 2016.

4. These provinces are Adiyaman, Agri, Ardahan, Batman, Bingol, Bitlis, Diyarbakir, Elazig, Erzincan, Erzurum, Gaziantep, Hakkari, Hatay, Igdir, Kahramanmaras, Kars, Kilis, Malatya, Mardin, Mus, Sanliurfa, Siirt, Sirnak, Tunceli, and Van. Population data for each (NUTS3 level) province for 2015 are obtained from https://biruni.tuik.gov.tr/medas/?kn=95&locale=tr, accessed April 19, 2016.

5. Batman, for instance, a city on the eastern border of Diyarbakir and with a high level of support for the insurgency, made the headlines for women suicides related to the traumatic experiences caused by political violence in the 2000s (http://bianet.org/bianet/diger/132297-batman-da-sekiz-kadin).

CHAPTER 2

1. As Tripp (2015, 27) notes, not all violent conflicts produce the type of social and political change described in the existing literature. She concludes that civil wars or wars of national liberation are more likely to prompt social change than localized wars, proxy wars, or coups.

2. "Cumartesi Anneleri 600 haftadır aynı yerde" [Saturday Mothers Gather at the Same Place for 600 weeks] *Cumhuriyet*, September 24, 2016, http://www.cumhuriyet.com.tr/haber/turkiye/605030/Cumartesi_Anneleri_600_haftadir_ayni_yerde.html, accessed September 24, 2016.

3. Balcells (2012) examines the effects of wartime experiences on political identities and behavior using the case of the Spanish Civil War of 1936–1939 and finds that the outcome is heavily impacted by political cleavages (i.e., left-right) salient during the war.

4. Interview with the author, June 2015, Belgium.

5. Aspinal (2007, 2009) is a notable exception to which I return in detail in chapter 5.

CHAPTER 3

1. "The Women of the PKK." *Foreign Affairs*, June 3, 2015, https://www.foreignaffairs.com/photo-galleries/2015-06-03/women-pkk, accessed August 19, 2017.

2. This is similar to what social psychologist Michael Billig (1995) calls "banal nationalism," an endemic condition that is quietly reproduced in everyday contexts. While ubiquitous, banal nationalism is far from innocent or benign. It is the very foundation upon which harmful, frenzied forms of nationalism are built.

3. For a summary of this transformation see Akkaya and Jongerden (2011).

4. As noted in the introduction, the PKK and the ideology it has embraced have shown noticeable changes over the past four decades. My goal here is not to offer a detailed account of the group's ideology but rather to highlight aspects of this worldview that speak directly to gender-related issues as well as its effects on the process of secularization.

5. "Secimin Kazanin Kadinlari [The Women Winners of the Elections]" http://bianet.org/bianet/siyaset/154631-secimin-kazanan-kadinlari, accessed October 28, 2016.

6. The DTP was successor of the HADEP, shut down by the Turkish Constitutional Court on the grounds of having ties with the PKK.

7. The BDP was the successor of the DTP, banned in 2009 on the grounds that it had become a focal point of activities against the indivisible unity of the state.

8. It should be noted, however, that women's participation in the PKK precedes the Fifth Congress and the changes it produced. The First Congress in 1978 included a female delegate, Sakine Cansiz, who would later become a role model for many women activists who joined the movement. Leyla Zana, the first Kurdish woman who was elected to parliament in 1991, serves as another example of women's role within the Kurdish movement prior to the establishment of an independent women's militia.

9. For a summary, see http://www.kjk-online.org/hakkimizda/?lang=en, accessed September 24, 2016.

10. The LTTE case in Sri Lanka offers a useful comparison. As Alison (2003, 45) argues, despite the LTTE's commitment to women's liberation, it is seen as secondary and "dependent on the struggle" for national liberation. The positive changes Alison describes in the roles and actions of women in the LTTE case are more of a result of the first mechanism outlined in chapter 2.

11. While this formulation is not particularly original and has been criticized for being "essentialist," it has nonetheless engendered noteworthy changes (Acik 2014). Al-Ali and Pratt (2011), drawing on the case of the Kurdish women's movement in Iraq, explore the complex relationship between nationalism and feminism and reach a similar conclusion that "nationalism per se is not an obstacle to women's rights in Iraqi Kurdistan."

12. These statistics are obtained from the Turkish Statistical Institute. https://biruni.tuik.gov.tr/secilmisgostergeler/degiskenlerUzerindenSorgula. do?durum=acKapa&menuNo=69&altMenuGoster=1&secilenDegiskenList esi=#, accessed September 29, 2016.

13. https://biruni.tuik.gov.tr/secilmisgostergeler/anaSayfa.do?dil=en, accessed September 29, 2016.

14. Unless noted otherwise, all interviews were conducted by the author between December 2013 and August 2016.

15. This variable is significant at the 0.07 level. In light of theoretical arguments and findings in the existing literature, however, the use of a one-tail test is justified and would have provided a significance level of 0.035. Thus the positive coefficient on this variable is in line with the hypothesized effect of armed conflict on developing positive attitudes toward women.

16. I re-examined the data with a trichotomous variable that distinguishes "no exposure" category from "direct" and "indirect" exposure categories. The use of such an alternative categorization yielded very similar results. Since I am mainly interested in tackling the relationship between direct exposure and the social and political outcomes outlined in this book, I use a dichotomous variable.

17. I also used an instrumental variable two-stage least squares (IV-2SLS) estimation to account for an endogenous relationship between the outcome and primary explanatory variables. Results from these models, using "voting for the BDP" as an instrument, showed that the first-stage relationship between support for the BDP and exposure to violence is strongly positive. Results from the second-stage, however, confirmed the effect of war-related violence on having positive attitudes toward women.

18. I also examined the data by accounting for potential qualitative differences between the three provinces. An analysis of the data by adding dummy variables to control for differences between the three provinces shows that respondents from Sanliurfa and Van provinces had a significantly lower level

of support for women as leaders than those from Diyarbakir, the province with the highest rate of exposure to violence and support for pro-Kurdish political parties. With some minor changes, the findings from these alternative models confirmed the main findings reported in tables 5 and 6.

CHAPTER 4

1. It is worth mentioning that the effect of the "age" variable on the three main outcomes examined in this book is not clear-cut or consistent. Older respondents appear to be more supportive of women as leaders (tables 5 and 6). The relationship between age and support for democracy seems to be sensitive to the choice of statistical method (models 1 and 2 of table 10). The effect of this variable on predicting support for the national government, the judiciary, and the local governance is not discernible (models 3–5 of table 10). Similarly, results from tables 12 and 13 do not paint a consistent picture on the effect of "age" on religiosity. While it has no noticeable effect on "importance" in table 12, the negative coefficient on this variable in table 13 (models 1 and 2) indicates a lesser religiosity for older respondents. The "age" variable is associated with a higher probability of daily prayer in both model 3 of table 12 and model 4 of table 13. Finally, the results reported in model 5 of table 13 indicate that older respondents are more likely to "agree" with the statement that "Whenever science and religion conflict, religion is always right" but not in model 4 of table 12. While this might be a result of measurement and data issues, it is in line with studies that have pointed out the "deeply concerning" effect of age on several outcomes, including support for democracy and trust in political institutions (Foa and Mounk 2016, 7).

2. The HudaPar participated in the March 30, 2014, local elections and received around 90,000 votes, representing 0.2 percent of votes cast nationwide. More than half of its total votes came from two Kurdish provinces, Diyarbakir (33,196) and Batman (13,206). The withdrawal of the HudaPar contributed to the AKP winning an additional seat from Diyarbakir in the November 2015 general elections.

3. Ahmet Turk won the elections in Mardin as an independent candidate. He was endorsed and supported by the BDP.

CHAPTER 5

1. For a more recent and detailed account of Kurdish Hizbullah see Kurt (2017).

2. HudaPar'in Rakibi BDP mi, AK Parti mi? [Who Is HudaPar's Rival? Is It the BDP or the AKP?] http://www.timeturk.com/tr/2012/12/06/partile-sen-hizbullah-cemaatinin-yapisi-degil.html, June 12, 2012, accessed May 15, 2016.

3. These data were obtained from the Ministry of National Education of the Republic of Turkey. http://sgb.meb.gov.tr/istatistik/meb_istatis tikleri_orgun_egitim_2012_2013.pdf. http://sgb.meb.gov.tr/meb_iys_dosya lar/2016_03/30044345_meb_istatistikleri_orgun_egitim_2015_2016.pdf, accessed May 16, 2016. These numbers do not include 1,961 junior (*orta*) Imam Hatip schools.

4. The Kurdish regions include the following provinces: Agri, Adiyaman, Ardahan, Batman, Bingol, Bitlis, Diyarbakir, Elazig, Hakkari, Igdir, Kars, Mardin, Mus, Sirnak, Sanliurfa, Siirt, Tunceli, and Van. Fifteen of these provinces have at least 40 percent Kurdish population. Ardahan, Igdir, and Kars provinces, despite a smaller ratio of Kurdish population, are included due to the strong showing of the pro-Kurdish Peoples' Democratic Party (HDP) in the most recent Turkish parliamentary elections. The data on Kurdish population was obtained from Mutlu (1996). Mutlu utilizes the data from the 1965 census, which is the last census that collected data on the percentage of people who spoke Kurdish (or Zazaki) as their primary language, to predict the ratio of Kurdish population in 1990.

5. The data on education are from the Ministry of National Education. http://sgb.meb.gov.tr/meb_iys_dosyalar/2016_03/30044345_meb_istatis tikleri_orgun_egitim_2015_2016.pdf, accessed May 16, 2016.

6. *Hurriyet*, April 17, 2016, http://www.hurriyet.com.tr/erdogan-babama-laz-miyiz-turk-muyuz-diye-sordum-40089936, accessed October 31, 2016.

7. http://www.mynet.com/haber/politika/basbakan-davutoglu-bayram-namazini-diyarbakirda-kildi-2088586-1, September 24, 2015, accessed March 7, 2017.

8. The Turkish viewpoint deliberately minimized the nationalistic character and emphasized its religious aspect. The portrayal of the rebellion as solely a religious attempt by reactionary forces against the modern Turkish Republic runs counter to the words of the prosecutors of the special courts-martial created to try and punish the perpetrators. The prosecutor, in summing up the case against Shaik Said and his collaborators, concluded: "Some of you induced by personal egoism, others by foreign council and political jealousies, but all of you motivated by the purpose to set up an independent Kurdish state, started the revolution" (Jwaideh 2006, 207–9).

CHAPTER 6

1. United Nations Press Release, DSG/SM 337, September 6, 2007, http://www.un.org/press/en/2007/dsgsm337.doc.htm, accessed December 1, 2016.

2. The initial annual death criterion of a minimum of one thousand battle-related fatalities a year was first proposed by the Correlates of War (COW) Project in the 1970s (Sarkees and Wayman 2010). This coding rule, however, was later criticized by others to be too high. Fearon and Laitin (2003) use

one hundred deaths a year, whereas Sambanis (2004), pointing out issues with using a single cutoff point, argues for a range of five hundred to one thousand deaths to code a civil war. Another widely used dataset, the Uppsala Conflict Data Program/Peace Research Institute in Oslo (UCDP/PRIO) Armed Conflict Dataset, employs a much lower threshold, twenty-five annual battle deaths (Gleditsch et al. 2002).

3. These events, often characterized as genocide, resulted in an estimated two million Armenian and Assyrian deaths (Rafter 2016, 229).

4. The detrimental effect language has on socioeconomic development is striking. As Laitin and Ramachandran (2016, 458) summarize, "if a country like Zambia were to adopt Mambwe instead of English as its official language, it would move up 44 positions on the HDI ranking and become similar to a country like Paraguay in human developments levels."

5. "Millions Gather in Istanbul for Raucous Democracy Rally," *Deutsche Welle*, August 7, 2016, http://www.dw.com/en/millions-gather-in-istanbul-for-raucous-democracy-rally/a-19455006, accessed December 1, 2016. It is also worth mentioning that the alleged mastermind of the failed military coup—Fethullah Gulen and his network of thousands in the Turkish police, army, and judiciary—was not only a close ally of the Turkish president and his AKP until they turned on each other in 2011, but also was responsible for detaining and arresting thousands of Kurdish human rights activists on largely made-up charges.

6. Saracoglu (2009) conceptualizes these sentiments as "exclusive recognition," producing and reproducing the negative perception of Kurdishness in the Turkish urban space.

7. The goal here is to highlight cultural impediments to peace, not to categorically deny the presence of many liberal minded pro-democracy Turks, some of whom have paid a high price for calling for a peaceful coexistence with the Kurds. It should be noted the HDP's electoral success on June 7, 2015, was in part driven by this small albeit significant group's support for the party as a way of curtailing Islamist AKP's power.

8. Volkan, ignoring the century-long ban on the Kurdish language as a factor that explains why today many Kurds cannot speak Kurdish, voices the widespread state propaganda that the PKK leader does not speak Kurdish. Notwithstanding several examples of nationalist leaders who could not speak or were not fluent in the language of the people they claimed to represent (e.g., Zionist leader Theodor Herzl, the Algerian Ferhat Abbas, and Irish nationalist leaders, see, for instance, Neuberger 2014, 21), the PKK leader in fact is fluent in Kurdish.

9. Barkey and Fuller (1997, 60) estimate the yearly direct cost of the conflict at anywhere between 2 and 3 percent of the Turkish GDP. This figure does not include indirect costs such as the opportunity cost of insurrection, lost tourism revenues, or lost industrial output. Costalli, Moretti, and Pischedda (2017)

examine the war-induced economic costs and find an annual average loss of about 2 percent GDP per capita in Turkey due to the Kurdish conflict. While this figure appears to be lower than the annual average loss of 17.5 percent of GDP per capita for the twenty war-torn countries included in the study, the authors warn that the limited impact may be due to the fact that the conflict might have disproportionally affected the Kurdish southeast. They observe a decline of about 12 percent of GDP per capita for the years 1997–1999, one of the most intense time periods in the conflict.

10. Ergin (2014, 323), pointing out the changing nature of Kurdish question, argues that Kurdishness in Turkey is "in the process of acquiring racial characteristics," dashing hopes of peaceful coexistence between the two peoples.

11. "6–7 Ekimin'in Aci Bilancosu" [The Sad Toll of 6–7 October], *Hurriyet*, November 6, 2014, http://www.hurriyet.com.tr/6-7-ekim-in-aci-bilancosu-50-olu-27525777, accessed September 6, 2016.

12. While the PKK insurgency is often referred to as the "29th Kurdish rebellion," Mehmet Ali Birand, a veteran journalist, citing a report from a retired Turkish army officer, lists at least thirty-seven Kurdish rebellions since the early nineteenth century, twenty-four of which occurred after 1920. "Bugune Kadar Kac Kurt Isyani Oldu" [How Many Kurdish Rebellions Have Occurred?], *Hurriyet*, January 2, 2008, http://www.hurriyet.com.tr/bugune-kadar-kac-kurt-isyani-oldu-7957402, accessed April 4, 2017.

13. "Questions and Answers about the Democratic Opening Process: The National Unity and Brotherhood Project" January 2010, http://www.akparti.org.tr/upload/documents/acilim22011011.pdf, accessed December 13, 2016.

14. As of April 2017, the government had jailed thirteen HDP members of parliament on terrorism charges, detained more than five thousand HDP party officials, and seized the vast majority of all municipalities (82 out of 103) won by the Kurdish party in the 2014 local elections (Phillips 2017).

15. "Trustee Removes Monument Built after Uludere Incident in Southeastern Turkey," *Hurriyet Daily News*, January 9, 2017, http://www.hurriyetdaily news.com/trustee-removes-monument-built-after-uludere-incident-in-south eastern-turkey.aspx?pageID=238&nID=108304&NewsCatID=341, accessed January 23, 2017. For a detailed account of the incident, widely referred to as the Roboski Massacre especially among the Kurds, see Geerdink (2015).

CHAPTER 7

1. This is in line with studies that have pointed to the link between leftist ideology and gains in women's rights at the country level (Hughes and Paxton 2008; Thames and Williams 2015).

2. The PJAK (Party of Free Life of Kurdistan in Iran) and People's Mujahedeen of Iran (commonly referred to the Mujahedeen-e-Khalq, or MEK) are also listed within this category. It should be noted that the PJAK is often con-

sidered to be an "extension" of or "inspired" by the PKK. Although the MEK has engaged in a low-intensity conflict against Iran since 1979, it neither poses a significant threat to the regime nor does it have a sizable social base in Iran. The UCDP Conflict Termination dataset treats the MEK case as "inactive," failing to fulfill the criteria used to code a conflict (Kreutz 2010).

3. "Armenian, Assyrian Writing Removed from Sur Municipality Building in Diyarbakir," *The Armenian Weekly*, December 9, 2016, http://armenianweekly.com/2016/12/09/armenian-assyrian-writing-removed/, accessed December 9, 2016.

Bibliography

Acik, Necla. 2014. "Redefining the Role of Women within the Kurdish National Movement in Turkey in the 1990s." In *The Kurdish Question in Turkey: New Perspectives on Violence, Representation, and Reconciliation*, edited by Cengiz Gunes and Welat Zeydanlioglu, 114–36. London: Routledge.

Adhikari, Prakash. 2013. "Conflict-Induced Displacement, Understanding the Causes of Flight." *American Journal of Political Science* 57 (1): 82–89.

Ahmed, Leila. 1982. "Feminism and Feminist Movements in the Middle East, a Preliminary Exploration: Turkey, Egypt, Algeria, People's Democratic Republic of Yemen." *Women's Studies International Forum* 5 (2): 153–68.

Akat, Ayla, Nadje Al-Ali, and Latif Tas. 2016. "Kurds and Turks Are at the Edge of a Cliff." *Open Democracy*, November 2, 2016, https://www.opendemocracy.net/nadje-al-ali-latif-tas-ayla-akat/kurds-and-turks-are-at-edge-of-cliff, accessed November 15, 2016.

Akkaya, Ahmet Hamdi, and Joost Jongerden. 2011. "The PKK in the 2000s: Continuity Through Breaks?" In *Nationalisms and Politics in Turkey: Political Islam, Kemalism and the Kurdish Issue*, edited by Marlies Casier and Joost Jongerden, 143–62. London: Routledge.

Akkaya, Ahmet Hamdi, and Joost Jongerden. 2014. "Confederalism and Autonomy in Turkey: The Kurdistan Workers' Party and the Reinvention of Democracy." In *The Kurdish Question in Turkey: New Perspectives on Violence, Representation, and Reconciliation*, edited by Cengiz Gunes and Welat Zeydanlioglu, 186–204. London: Routledge, 186–204.

Akturk, Sener. 2015. "Religion and Nationalism: Contradictions of Islamic Origins and Secular Nation-Building in Turkey, Algeria, and Pakistan." *Social Science Quarterly* 96 (3): 778–806.

Al-Ali, Nadje, and Nicola Pratt. 2011. "Between Nationalism and Women's Rights: The Kurdish Women's Movement in Iraq." *Middle East Journal of Culture and Communication* 4: 337–53.

Alison, Miranda. 2003. "Cogs in the Wheel? Women in the Liberation Tigers of Tamil Eelam." *Civil Wars* 6 (4): 37–54.

Alison, Miranda. 2004. "Women as Agents of Political Violence: Gendering Security." *Security Dialogue* 35 (4): 447–63.

Anderson, Benedict. 2006. *Imagined Communities: Reflections on the Origin and Spread of Nationalism*. London: Verso.

Anderson, Lisa. 1987. "The State in the Middle East and North Africa." *Comparative Politics* 20 (1): 1–18.

Appleby, R. Scott. 2000. *The Ambivalence of the Sacred: Religion, Violence, and Reconciliation*. Lanham, MD: Rowman & Littlefield.

Arat, Yesim. 2010. "Religion, Politics and Gender Equality in Turkey: Implications of a Democratic Paradox?" *Third World Quarterly* 31 (6): 869–84.

Arendt, Hannah. 1969. *On Violence*. New York: Harcourt, Brace & World.

Arendt, Hannah. 1990. *On Revolution*. London: Penguin Books.

Argentieri, Benedetta. 2015. "One Group Battling Islamic State Has a Secret Weapon—Female Fighters." *Reuters*, February 3, 2015, http://blogs.reuters.com/great-debate/2015/02/03/the-pro-woman-ideology-battling-islamic-state/, accessed August 4, 2016.

Arifcan, Umut. 1997. "The Saturday Mothers of Turkey." *Peace Review* 9 (2): 265–72, DOI: 10.1080/10402659708426062.

Armstrong, Karen. 2014. *Fields of Blood: Religion and the History of Violence*. New York: Alfred A. Knopf.

Armey, Laura E., and Robert M. McNab. 2015. "Democratization and Civil War." *Applied Economics* 47 (18): 1863–82.

Asik, Gunes A. 2012. "TÜRKİYE'DE KADINLARIN İŞGÜCÜNE KATI-LIMI: İstanbul ve Ankara'da Katılım, Bingöl ve Tunceli ile Aynı" [Women's Participation in the Labor Force: Istanbul and Ankara Have the Same Rate as Bingol and Tunceli], http://www.tepav.org.tr/tr/ekibimiz/s/1274/Gunes+A.+Asik, accessed September 29, 2016.

Aslan, Senem. 2007. "'Citizen Speak Turkish!': A Nation in the Making." *Nationalism and Ethnic Politics* 13 (2): 245–72.

Aspinall, Edward. 2007. "From Islamism to Nationalism in Aceh, Indonesia." *Nations and Nationalism* 13 (2): 245–63.

Aspinall, Edward. 2009. *Islam and Nation: Separatist Rebellion in Aceh, Indonesia*. Stanford, CA: Stanford University Press.

Aydin, Aysegul, and Cem Emrence. 2015. *Zones of Rebellion: Kurdish Insurgents and the Turkish State*. Ithaca, NY: Cornell University Press.

Balcells, Laia. 2010. "Rivalry and Revenge: Violence Against Civilians in Conventional Civil Wars." *International Studies Quarterly* 54 (2): 291–313.

Balcells, Laia. 2012. "The Consequences of Victimization on Political Identities: Evidence from Spain." *Politics & Society* 40 (3): 311–47.

Balcells, Laia. 2017. *Rivalry and Revenge: The Politics of Violence during Civil War.* Cambridge: Cambridge University Press.

Barkey, J. Henri. 2014. "The Meaning of Kobani." *The American Interest*, October 18, http://www.the-american-interest.com/2014/10/18/the-meaning-of-kobani/, accessed February 13, 2017.

Barkey, J. Henri, and Graham E. Fuller. 1997. "Turkey's Kurdish Question: Critical Turning Points and Missed Opportunities." *Middle East Journal* 51 (1): 59–79.

Barkey, J. Henri, and Graham E. Fuller. 1998. *Turkey's Kurdish Question.* Lanham, MD: Rowman & Littlefield.

Basedau, Matthias, Georg Struver, Johannes Vullers, and Tim Wegenast. 2011. "Do Religious Factors Impact Armed Conflict? Empirical Evidence From Sub-Saharan Africa." *Terrorism and Political Violence* 23 (5): 752–79.

Bateson, Regina. 2012. "Crime Victimization and Political Participation." *American Political Science Review* 106 (3): 570–87.

Baydar, Gulsum, and Berfin Ivegen. 2006. "Territories, Identities, and Thresholds: The Saturday Mothers Phenomenon in Istanbul." *Signs: Journal of Women in Culture and Society* 31 (3): 689–715.

Bayer, Resat, and Matthew C. Rupert. 2004. "Effects of Civil War on International Trade." *Journal of Peace Research* 41 (6): 699–713.

Bayir, Derya. 2013. *Minorities and Nationalism in Turkish Law.* London and New York: Routledge.

Belge, Ceren, and Ekrem Karakoc. 2015. "Minorities in the Middle East: Ethnicity, Religion, and Support for Authoritarianism." *Political Research Quarterly* 68 (2): 280–92.

Bellows, John, and Edward Miguel. 2009. "War and Local Collective Action in Sierra Leone." *Journal of Public Economics* 93: 1144–57.

Benford, Robert D., and David A. Snow. 2000. "Framing Processes and Social Movements: An Overview and Assessment." *Annual Review of Sociology* 26: 611–39.

Bengio, Ofra. 2016. "Game Changers: Kurdish Women in Peace and War." *The Middle East Journal* 70 (1): 30–46.

Bengio, Ofra. 2017. "Separated but Connected: The Synergic Effects in the Kurdistan Sub-System." In *The Kurdish Question Revisited*, edited by Gareth Stansfield and Mohammed Shareef, 77–91. London: Hurst Publishers.

Billig, Michael. 1995. *Banal Nationalism.* London: Sage.

Blattman, Christopher. 2009. "From Violence to Voting: War and Political Participation in Uganda." *American Political Science Review* 103 (2): 231–47.

Blumberg, Rae Lesser. 2001. "Risky Business: What Happens to Gender Equality and Women's Rights in Post-Conflict Societies? Insights from

NGOs in El Salvador." *International Journal of Politics, Culture and Society* 15 (1): 161–73.

Booth, John A., and Mitchell A. Seligson. 2009. *The Legitimacy Puzzle in Latin America: Political Support and Democracy in Eight Latin American Nations.* New York: Cambridge University Press.

Bormann, Nils-Christian, Lars-Erik Cederman, and Manuel Vogt. 2017. "Language, Religion, and Ethnic Civil War." *Journal of Conflict Resolution* 61 (4): 744–71.

Bownas, Richard A. 2015. "Dalits and Maoists in Nepal's Civil War: Between Synergy and Co-optation." *Contemporary South Asia* 23 (4): 409–25.

Bozarslan, Hamit. 2017. "'Being in Time': The Kurdish Movement and Universal Quests." In *The Kurdish Question Revisited*, edited by Gareth Stansfield and Mohammed Shareef, 61–75. London: Hurst Publishers.

Bozarslan, Mahmut. 2017. "Is Turkey Wiping Out Kurdish Institutions During Lengthy State of Emergency." *Al-Monitor*, January 11, 2017, http://www.al-monitor.com/pulse/originals/2017/01/turkey-emergency-rule-wipe-out-kurdish-institutions.html, accessed January 13, 2017.

Brauer, Jurgen. 2009. *War and Nature: The Environmental Consequences of War in a Globalized World.* Plymouth, UK: AltaMira Press.

Britzman, Deborah P. 2000. "If the Story Cannot End: Deferred Action, Ambivalence, and Difficult Knowledge." In *Between Hope and Despair: Pedagogy and the Remembrance of Historical Trauma*, edited by Roger I. Simon, Sharon Rosenberg, and Claudia Eppert, 27–55. Lanham, MD: Rowman & Littlefield.

Brodzinsky, Sibylla. 2016. "FARC Rebels Prepare to Leave Behind Guns, Drug Trade and the Life They Know." *The Huffington Post*, September 28, 2016, http://www.huffingtonpost.com/entry/farc-ceasefire_us_57e03c2ae4b08cb140974a89, accessed October 3, 2016.

Brogan, Walter A. 1988. "The Central Significance of Suffering in Nietzsche's Thought." *International Studies in Philosophy* 20 (2): 53–62.

Brown, L. Carl. 2000. *Religion and State: The Muslim Approach to Politics.* New York: Columbia University Press.

Brubaker, Rogers. 2009. "Ethnicity, Race and Nationalism." *Annual Review of Sociology* 35 (1): 21–42.

Bruinessen, Martin van. 1992. *Agha, Shaikh and State: The Social and Political Structures of Kurdistan.* London, UK: Zed Books.

Bruinessen, Martin van. 1999. *The Kurds and Islam.* Islamic Area Studies Working Paper Series No. 13. Tokyo, Japan.

Buhaug, Halvard, Lars-Erik Cederman, and Jan Ketil Rød. 2008. "Disaggregating Ethno-Nationalist Civil Wars: A Dyadic Test of Exclusion Theory." *International Organization* 62 (Summer): 531–51.

Butler, Daren. 2013. "Slain Kurdish Activist Cansiz Leaves Stamp on Militant PKK." *Reuters*, January 11, 2013, http://www.reuters.com/article/us-france-kurds-cansiz-idUSBRE90A0Z120130111, accessed September 24, 2016.

Button, James W. 1989. *Blacks and Social Change: Impacts of the Civil Rights Movement in Southern Communities*. Princeton, NJ: Princeton University Press.

Caglayan, Handan. 2010. *Analar, Yoldaşlar, Tanrıçalar: Kürt Hareketinde Kadınlar ve Kadın Kimliğinin İnşası* (Mothers, Comrades, Goddesses: Women in the Kurdish Movement and the Formation of Women's Identity). Istanbul: Iletisim.

Caglayan, Handan. 2012. "From Kawa the Blacksmith to Ishtar the Goddess: Gender Constructions in Ideological-Political Discourses of the Kurdish Movement in Post-1980 Turkey." *European Journal of Turkish Studies* [Online] 14, http://ejts.revues.org/4657.

Cagaptay, Soner. 2004. "Race, Assimilation and Kemalism: Turkish Nationalism and the Minorities in the 1930s." *The Middle Eastern Studies* 40 (3): 86–101.

Cakir, Rusen. 2007. "The Emergence of Hizballah in Turkey." *Washington Institute*, September 2007, http://www.washingtoninstitute.org/uploads/Documents/pubs/PolicyFocus74initial.pdf, accessed May 15, 2016.

Caldwell, John C. 1982. *Theory of Fertility Decline*. London: Academic Press.

Calhoun, Craig, Mark Juergensmeyer, and Jonathan VanAntwerpen. 2011. "Introduction." In *Rethinking Secularism*, edited by Craig Calhoun, Mark Juergensmeyer, and Jonathan VanAntwerpen, 3–30. Oxford: Oxford University Press.

Calislar, Oral. 2015. "Why Does Turkey Say PYD Is More Dangerous than IS?" *Al-Monitor*, June 22, 2015, http://www.al-monitor.com/pulse/security/2015/06/turkey-syria-pyd-more-dangerous-isis.html, accessed December 12, 2016.

Canetti-Nisim, Daphna, Eran Halperin, Keren Sharvit, and Stevan E. Hobfoll. 2009. "A New Stress-Based Model of Political Extremism: Personal Exposure to Terrorism, Psychological Distress, and Exclusionist Political Attitudes." *Journal of Conflict Resolution* 53 (3): 363–89.

Caruth, Cathy. 1996. *Unclaimed Experience: Trauma, Narrative, and History*. Baltimore: Johns Hopkins University Press.

Casanova, Jose. 2011. "The Secular, Secularizations, Secularisms." In *Rethinking Secularism*, edited by Craig Calhoun, Mark Juergensmeyer, and Jonathan VanAntwerpen, 54–74. Oxford: Oxford University Press.

Cederman, Lars Erik, Kristian Skrede Gleditsch, Idean Salehyan, and Julian Wucherpfennig. 2013. "Transborder Ethnic Kin and Civil War." *International Organization* 67 (Spring): 389–410.

Cederman, Lars-Erik, Andreas Wimmer, and Brian Min. 2010. "Why Do Ethnic Groups Rebel: New Data and Analysis." *World Politic* 62 (1): 87–119.

Celik, A. Betul. 2005. "'I miss my village!': Forced Kurdish Migrants in Istanbul and Their Representation in Associations." *New Perspectives on Turkey* 32: 137–163.

Cengiz, Orhan Kemal. "Erdogan's Reforms Meant to Educate 'Pious Genera-
    tion,,'" *Al-Monitor*, June 26, 2014, http://www.al-monitor.com/pulse/origi
    nals/2014/06/cengiz-produce-religious-generations-erdogan-akp-islamist.
    html, accessed October 25, 2016.
Chafe, H. William. 1999. *The Unfinished Journey: America Since World War I.*
    New York: Oxford University Press.
Chamarbagwala, Rubina, and Hilcias E. Moran. 2011. "The Human Capital
    Consequences of Civil War: Evidence from Guatemala." *Journal of Develop-
    ment Economics* 94 (1): 41–61.
Chapman, Thomas, and Philip Roeder. 2007. "Partition as a Solution to Wars
    of Nationalism: The Importance of Institutions." *American Political Science
    Review* 101 (4): 677 91.
Chong, Dennis. 1991. *Collective Action and the Civil Rights Movement.* Chicago:
    University of Chicago Press.
Christie, J. Clive. 1992. "Partition, Separatism, and National Identity: A Reas-
    sessment." *Political Quarterly* 63 (1): 68–78.
Christie, J. Clive. 1996. *A Modern History of Southeast Asia: Decolonization,
    Nationalism and Separatism.* I. B. Tauris: London and New York.
Cicek, Cuma. 2011. "Elimination or Integration of Pro-Kurdish Politics: Lim-
    its of the AKP's Democratic Initiative." *Turkish Studies* 12 (1): 15–26.
Clark, Bruce. 2006. *Twice a Stranger: The Mass Expulsions that Forged Modern
    Greece and Turkey.* Cambridge, MA: Harvard University Press.
Cockburn, Cynthia. 2007. *From Where We Stand: War, Women's Activism and
    Feminist Analysis.* London: Zed Publishers.
Cohen, Nissim, and Tamar Arieli. 2011. "Field Research in Conflict Environ-
    ments: Methodological Challenges and Snowball Sampling." *Journal of
    Peace Research* 48 (4): 423–35.
Cohen, Roberta, and Francis M. Deng. 1998. *Masses in Flight: The Global Crisis
    of Internal Displacement.* Washington, DC: The Brookings Institution.
Collier, Paul. 1999. "On the Economic Consequences of Civil War." *Oxford
    Economic Papers* 51 (1): 168–83.
Collier, Paul, Lani Elliot, Havard Hegre, Ane Hoeffler, Nicholas Sambanis,
    and Marta Reynal-Querol. 2003. *Breaking the Conflict Trap: Civil War and
    Development Policy.* Oxford, UK: Oxford University Press.
Collier, Paul, and Anke Hoeffler. 2004. "Greed and Grievance in Civil War."
    Oxford Economic Papers 56 (4): 563–95.
Conteh, Prince Sorie. 2011. "The Role of Religion During and After the Civil
    War in Sierra Leone." *Journal for the Study of Religion* 24 (1): 55–76.
Cook, A. Steven. 2016. "'How Happy Is the One Who Says, I Am a Turk.'"
    Foreign Policy, March 28, 2016, http://foreignpolicy.com/2016/03/28/how-
    happy-is-the-one-who-says-i-am-a-turk/, accessed November 29, 2016.
Costalli, Stefano, Luigi Moretti, and Costantino Pischedda. 2017. "The
    Economic Costs of Civil War: Synthetic Counterfactual Evidence and

the Effects of Ethnic Fractionalization." *Journal of Peace Research* 54 (1): 80–98.

Cramer, Christopher. 2006. *Civil War Is Not a Stupid Thing: Accounting for Violence in Developing Countries*. London: Hurst & Company.

Crick, Bernard. 2002. *Democracy: A Very Short Introduction*. New York: Oxford University Press.

Dahl, A. Robert. 1998. *On Democracy*. New Haven, CT: Yale University Press.

Davies, James C. 1962. "Toward a Theory of Revolution." *American Sociological Review* 27 (1): 5–19.

Dearden, Lizzie. 2014. "'Women Should Not Laugh in Public,' says Turkey's Deputy Prime Minister in Morality Speech." *The Independent*, July 29, 2014, http://www.independent.co.uk/news/world/europe/women-should-not-laugh-in-public-says-turkeys-deputy-prime-minister-in-morality-speech-9635526.html, accessed October 3, 2016.

Dobbelaere, Karel. 1999. "Towards an Integrated Perspective of the Processes Related to the Descriptive Concept of Secularization." *Sociology of Religion* 60 (3): 229–47.

Dobbelaere, Karel. 2002. *Secularization: An Analysis at Three Levels*. Brussels, Belgium: P.I.E.—Peter Lang.

Dobbelaere, Karel. 2007. "Testing Secularization Theory in Comparative Perspective." *Nordic Journal of Religion and Society* 20 (2): 137–47.

Doyle, Michael, and Nicholas Sambanis. 2000. "International Peacebuilding: A Theoretical and Quantitative Analysis." *American Political Science Review* 94 (4): 779–801.

Driessen, D. Michael. 2010. "Religion, State, and Democracy: Analyzing Two Dimensions of Church-State Arrangements." *Politics and Religion* 3 (1): 55–80.

Driessen, D. Michael. 2014. *Religion and Democratization: Framing Religious and Political Identities in Muslim and Catholic Societies*. New York: Oxford University Press.

Drwish, Sardar Mlla. "After Approving Constitution, What's Next for Syria's Kurds?" *Al-Monitor*, July 22, 2016, http://www.al-monitor.com/pulse/orig inals/2016/07/north-syria-rojava-kurdish-federation-constitution.html, accessed September 8, 2016.

Eccarius-Kelly, Vera. 2016. "Behind the Front Lines: Kobani, Legitimacy, and Kurdish Diaspora Mobilization." In *Kurdish Issues: Essays in Honor of Robert W. Olson*, edited by Michael M. Gunter, 40–61. Costa Mesa, CA: Mazda Publishers.

Elbadawi, Ibrahim, and Nicholas Sambanis. 2000. "Why Are There So Many Civil Wars in Africa? Understanding and Preventing Violent Conflict." *Journal of African Economics* 9 (3): 244–69.

Englebert, Pierre. 2000. *State Legitimacy and Development in Africa*. Boulder, CO: Lynne Rienner.

Enzinna, Wes. 2015. "A Dream of Secular Utopia in ISIS' Backyard." *The New York Times*, November 24, 2015, http://www.nytimes.com/2015/11/29/magazine/a-dream-of-utopia-in-hell.html, accessed March 27, 2016.

Ergin, Murat. 2014. "The Racialization of Kurdish Identity in Turkey." *Ethnic and Racial Studies* 37 (2): 322–41.

Eriksson, Mikael, Peter Wallenstteen, and Margareta Sollenberg. 2003. "Armed Conflict, 1989–2002." *Journal of Peace Research* 40 (5): 593–607.

Etten, Jacob van, Joost Jongerden, Hugo J. de Vos, Annemarie Klaasse, and Esther C. E. van Hoeve. 2008. "Environmental Destruction as Counterinsurgency Strategy in the Kurdistan Region of Turkey." *Geoforum* 39 (5): 1786–97.

Fahim, Kareem. 2016. "Yemen's War Becomes the Mother of Reinvention." *The New York Times*, May 18, 2016, http://www.nytimes.com/2016/05/19/world/middleeast/yemen-war-solar-power-economy.html?smprod=nytcore-iphonc&smid=nytcore-iphone-share&_r=1&mtrref=undefined, accessed August 10, 2016.

Fanon, Frantz. 2004. *The Wretched of the Earth*. New York: Grove Press.

Fearon, James D., and David D. Laitin. 1996. "Explaining Interethnic Cooperation." *American Political Science Review* 90 (4): 715–35.

Fearon, James D., and David D. Laitin. 2000. "Violence and the Social Construction of Ethnic Identity." *International Organization* 54 (4): 845–77.

Fearon, James D., and David D. Laitin. 2003. "Ethnicity, Insurgency, and Civil War." *American Political Science Review* 97 (1): 75–90.

Finer, Samuel E. 1975. "State- and Nation-Building in Europe: The Role of the Military." In *The Formation of National States in Western Europe*, edited by Charles Tilly, 84–163. Princeton, NJ: Princeton University Press.

Fish, M. Steven. 2002. "Islam and Authoritarianism." *World Politics* 55 (1): 4–37.

Foa, Roberto Stefan, and Yascha Mounk. 2016. "The Danger of Deconsolidation: The Democratic Disconnect." *Journal of Democracy* 27 (3): 5–17.

Fox, Jonathan. 1997. "The Salience of Religious Issues in Ethnic Conflicts: A Large-N Study." *Nationalism and Ethnic Politics* 3 (3): 1–19.

Fox, Jonathan. 2000. "The Ethnic-Religious Nexus: The Impact of Religion on Ethnic Conflict." *Civil Wars* 3 (3): 1–22.

Frankl, Viktor E. 1985. *Men's Search for Meaning*. New York: Washington Square Press.

Freire, Paulo. 2000. *Pedagogy of the Oppressed*. New York: Continuum.

Fujii, Lee Ann. 2010. "Shades of Truth and Lies: Interpreting Testimonies of War and Violence." *Journal of Peace Research* 47 (2): 231–41.

Galtung, Johan. 1969. "Violence, Peace, and Peace Research." *Journal of Peace Research* 6 (3): 167–91.

Galtung, Johan. 1985. "Twenty-Five Years of Peace Research: The Challenges and Some Responses." *Journal of Peace Research* 22 (2): 141–58.

Gelner, Ernest. 1992. *Postmodernism, Reason and Religion*. New York: Routledge.

Geerdink, Frederike. 2015. *The Boys Are Dead: The Roboski Massacre and the Kurdish Question in Turkey*. London: Gomidas Institute.

Ghobarah, Hazem Adam, Paul Huth, and Bruce Russet. 2003. "Civil Wars Kill and Maim People—Long After the Shooting Stops." *American Political Science Review* 97 (2): 189–202.

Gibson, James L. 1988. "Political Intolerance and Political Repression During the McCarthy Red Scare." *The American Political Science Review* 82 (2): 511–29.

Gibson, James L. 2004. "Does Truth Lead to Reconciliation? Testing the Causal Assumptions of the South African Truth and Reconciliation Process." *American Journal of Political Science* 48 (2): 201–17.

Gilligan, J. Michael, Benjamin J. Pasquale, and Cyrus Samii. 2014. "Civil War and Social Cohesion: Lab-in-the-Field Evidence from Nepal." *American Journal of Political Science* 58 (3): 604–19.

Gleditsch, Kristian Skrede. 2007. "Transnational Dimensions of Civil War." *Journal of Peace Research* 44 (3): 293–309.

Gleditsch, Nils Petter, Peter Wallensteen, Mikael Eriksson, Margareta Sollenberg, and Håvard Strand. 2002. "Armed Conflict 1946–2001: A New Dataset." *Journal of Peace Research* 39 (5): 615–37.

Glencorse, Blair, and Sujeev Shakya. 2015. "Shaking Up the Status Quo in Nepal." *The New York Times*, June 1, 2015, http://www.nytimes.com/2015/06/02/opinion/shaking-up-the-status-quo-in-nepal.html?ref=opinion&_r=0, accessed August 16, 2016.

Glover, Edward. 1935. *War, Sadism, and Pacifism*. London: Allen and Unwin.

Gocek, Fatma Muge. 1996. *Rise of the Bourgeoisie, Demise of Empire: Ottoman Westernization and Social Change*. New York: Oxford University Press.

Goldberg, M. Rachel, ed. 2016. *Faith & Practice in Conflict Resolution: Toward a Multidimensional Approach*. Boulder, CO: Kumarian Press.

Goldstone, Jack. 1998. "Social Movements or Revolutions? On the Evolution and Outcomes of Collective Action." In *From Contention to Democracy*, edited by Marco G. Giugni, Doug McAdam, and Charles Tilly, 125–48. Lanham, MD: Rowman & Littlefield.

Goodwin, Jeff, and Theda Skocpol. 1989. "Explaining Revolution in the Contemporary Third World." *Politics and Society* 17 (4): 489–509.

Gould, Stephen Jay. 1981. *The Mismeasure of Man*. New York: Norton & Company.

Graeber, David. 2014. "Why Is the World Ignoring the Revolutionary Kurds in Syria?" *The Guardian*, October 8, 2014, https://www.theguardian.com/commentisfree/2014/oct/08/why-world-ignoring-revolutionary-kurds-syria-isis, accessed August 18, 2016.

Grojean, Olivier. 2008. "The Production of New Man within the PKK." *European Journal of Turkish Studies* 8 (English translation 2014), http://ejts.revues.org/2753, accessed September 13, 2016.

Grosjean, Pauline. 2014. "Conflict and Social and Political Preferences: Evidence from World War II and Civil Conflict in 35 European Countries." *Comparative Economic Studies* 56 (3): 424–51.

Grossman, Guy, Devorah Manekin, and Dan Miodownik. 2015. "The Political Legacies of Combat: Attitudes Toward War and Peace Among Israeli Ex-Combatants." *International Organization* 69 (4): 981–1009.

Gubler, R. Joshua, and Joel Sawat Selway. 2012. "Horizontal Inequality, Cross-cutting Cleavages, and Civil War." *Journal of Conflict Resolution* 56 (2): 206–32.

Guelzo, Allen. 2015. "Did Religion Make the American Civil War Worse." *The Atlantic*, August 23, 2015, http://www.theatlantic.com/politics/archive/2015/08/did-religion-make-the-american-civil-war-worse/401633/?utm_source=atlfb, accessed October 25, 2016.

Guida, Michelangelo. 2008. "The Sèvres Syndrome and 'Komplo' Theories in the Islamist and Secular Press." *Turkish Studies* 9 (March): 37–52.

Gundogan, Dilay, and Emmabuelle Baillon. "Rise of Islamic Schools Causes Alarm in Secular Turkey," *The National*, September 21, 2014, http://www.thenational.ae/world/europe/rise-of-islamic-schools-causes-alarm-in-secular-turkey, accessed May 16, 2016.

Gunes, Cengiz. 2012. *Kurdish National Movement in Turkey: From Protest to Resistance*. London: Routledge.

Gunes, Cengiz. 2013. "Explaining the PKK's Mobilization of the Kurds in Turkey: Hegemony, Myth and Violence." *Ethnopolitics* 12 (3): 247–67.

Gunter, Michael. 2004. "The Kurdish Question in Perspective." *World Affairs* 166 (4): 197–205.

Gunter, Michael. 2016. *The Kurds: A Modern History*. Princeton, NJ: Markus Wiener Publishers.

Guo, Jeff. 2016. "Researchers Have Found that War Has Remarkable and Miraculous Effect" *Washington Post*, June 28, 2016, https://www.washingtonpost.com/news/wonk/wp/2016/06/28/researchers-have-found-that-war-has-a-remarkable-and-miraculous-effect/, accessed July 14, 2016.

Gurr, Ted Robert. 1970. *Why Men Rebel*. Princeton, NJ: Princeton University Pres.

Gurr, Ted Robert. 1973. "The Revolution–Social-Change Nexus: Some Old Theories and New Hypotheses." *Comparative Politics* 5 (3): 359–92.

Gurr, Ted Robert. 1993. Why Minorities Rebel: A Global Analysis of Communal Mobilization and Conflict since 1945." *International Political Science Review* 14 (2): 161–201.

Gurr, Ted Robert. 2012. "Some Observations on Resistance and Revolution in Contemporary Africa." *Journal of Asian and African Studies* 47 (3): 279–290.

Gurses, Mehmet. 2010. "Partition, Democracy, and Turkey's Kurdish Minority." *Nationalism and Ethnic Politics* 16 (3): 337–53.

Gurses, Mehmet. 2012. "Environmental Consequences of Civil War: Evidence from the Kurdish Conflict in Turkey." *Civil Wars* 14 (2): 254–71.

Gurses, Mehmet. 2014. "From War to Democracy: Transborder Kurdish Conflict and Democratization." In *Conflict, the Kurds, and Democratization in the Middle East: Turkey, Iran, Iraq, and Syria*, edited by David Romano and Mehmet Gurses, 249–65. New York: Palgrave Macmillan.

Gurses, Mehmet. 2015a. "Transnational Ethnic Kin and Civil War Outcome." *Political Research Quarterly* 68 (1): 142–53.

Gurses, Mehmet. 2015b. "Is Islam a Cure for Ethnic Conflict? Evidence from Turkey." *Politics and Religion* 8 (1): 135–54.

Gurses, Mehmet. 2015c. "Islamists and Women's Rights: Lessons from Turkey." *Journal of the Middle East and Africa* 6: 33–44.

Gurses, Mehmet. 2016. "Changing Civil War." *Mobilizing Ideas*, March 7, 2016, https://mobilizingideas.wordpress.com/2016/03/07/changing-civil-war/, accessed August 5, 2016.

Gurses, Mehmet, and T. David Mason. 2008. "Democracy Out of Anarchy: The Prospects for Post-Civil War Democracy." *Social Science Quarterly* 89 (2): 315–36.

Gurses, Mehmet, and David Mason. 2010. "Weak States, Regime Types, and Civil War." *Civil Wars* 12 (1): 140–55.

Gurses, Mehmet, and Nicolas Rost. 2013. "Sustaining the Peace after Ethnic Civil Wars." *Conflict Management and Peace Science* 30 (5): 469–91.

Gurses, Mehmet, and Nicolas Rost. 2016. "Religion as a Peacemaker? Peace Duration after Ethnic Civil Wars." *Religion and Politics* DOI: https://doi.org/10.1017/S1755048316000742.

Gutierrez-Sanin, Francisco, and Elisabeth Jean Wood. 2014. "Ideology in Civil War: Instrumental Adoption and Beyond." *Journal of Peace Research* 51 (2): 213–26.

Hall, Stuart. 1982. "The Rediscovery of 'Ideology': Return of the Repressed in Media Studies." In *Culture, Society and the Media*, edited by Michael Gurevitch, Tony Bennett, James Curran, and Janet Woolacott, 52–86. New York: Methuen.

Halpern, Jodi, and Harvey M. Weinstein. 2004. "Rehumanizing the Other: Empathy and Reconciliation." *Human Rights Quarterly* 26 (3): 561–83.

Harpviken, Kristian Berg, and Hanne Eggen Roislien. 2008. "Faithful Brokers? Potentials and Pitfalls of Religion in Peacemaking." *Conflict Resolution Quarterly* 25 (3): 351–73.

Haynes, Jeffrey. 2009. "Conflict, Conflict Resolution and Peace-Building: The Role of Religion in Mozambique, Nigeria and Cambodia." *Commonwealth & Comparative Politics* 47 (1): 52–75.

Hegre, Havard, and Nicholas Sambanis. 2006. "Sensitivity Analysis of Empirical Results on Civil War Onset." *Journal of Conflict Resolution* 50 (4): 508–35.

Hirschon, Renee, ed. 2003. *Crossing the Aegean: An Appraisal of the 1923 Compulsory Population Exchange between Greece and Turkey*. New York: Berghahn Books.

Hobsbawm, Eric. 1983. "Introduction: Inventing Traditions." In *The Invention of Tradition*, edited by Eric Hobsbawm and Terence Ranger, 1–14. Cambridge: Cambridge University Press.

Holmes, Amy Austin. 2015. "What Are the Kurdish Women's Units Fighting For in Syria?" *Washington Post*, December 23, 2015, https://www.washingtonpost.com/news/monkey-cage/wp/2015/12/23/what-are-the-kurdish-womens-units-fighting-for-in-syria/, accessed August 4, 2016.

Horowitz, Donald L. 1993. "The Challenge of Ethnic Conflict: Democracy in Divided Societies." *Journal of Democracy* 4 (4): 18–38.

Horowitz, Donald L. 2000. *Ethnic Groups in Conflict*. Berkeley: University of California Press.

Horowitz, Donald L. 2003. "The Cracked Foundations of the Right to Secede." *Journal of Democracy* 14 (2): 5–17.

Houston, Christopher. 2001. *Islam, Kurds and the Turkish Nation State*. New York: Berg.

Huang, Reyko. 2016. *The Wartime Origins of Democratization: Civil War, Rebel Governance, and Political Regimes*. Cambridge: Cambridge University Press.

Hughes, Melanie M., and Pamela Paxton. 2008. "Continuous Change, Episodes, and Critical Periods: A Framework for Understanding Women's Political Representation over Time." *Politics and Gender* 4 (2): 233–64.

Hughes, Melanie M., and Aili Mari Tripp. 2015. "Civil War and Trajectories of Change in Women's Political Participation in Africa, 1985–2010." *Social Forces* 93 (4): 1513–40.

Humphreys, Macartan. 2005. "Natural Resources, Conflict, and Conflict Resolution: Uncovering the Mechanisms." *Journal of Conflict Resolution* 49 (4): 508–37.

Humphreys, Macartan, and Jeremy M. Weinstein. 2008. "Who Fights? The Determinants of Participation in Civil War." *American Journal of Political Science* 52 (2): 436–55.

Huntington, Samuel. 1996. *The Clash of Civilizations and the Remaking of the World*. New York: Simon & Schuster.

Hur, Ayse. 2010. "Osmanli'dan Bugune Kurtler ve Devlet: Kurtlere Ozerklik Sozu Verildi mi?" [The Kurds and State since the Ottomans: Were the Kurds Promised Autonomy?] *Taraf*, May 17, 2010, http://www.cafrande.org/osmanlidan-bugune-kurtler-ve-devlet-kurtlere-ozerklik-sozu-verildi-mi-ayse-hur/, accessed December 11, 2016.

Hutchison, Emma. 2016. *Affective Communities in World Politics: Collective Emotions after Trauma*. Cambridge: Cambridge University Press.

Inglehart, Ronald, and Pippa Norris. 2003. "The True Clash of Civilizations." *Foreign Policy* 135 (March–April): 62–70.

Inkeles, Alex, and David H. Smith. 1974. *Becoming Modern: Individual Changes in Six Developing Countries*. Cambridge, MA: Harvard University Press.

Iqbal, Zaryab. 2006. "Health and Human Security: The Public Health Impact of Violent Conflict." *International Studies Quarterly* 50 (3): 631–49.

Jacoby, Tim, and Alpaslan Ozerdem. 2013. *Peace in Turkey 2023: The Question of Human Security and Conflict Transformation*. Lanham, MD: Lexington Books.

Johansen, C. Robert. 1997. "Radical Islam and Nonviolence: A Case Study of Religious Empowerment and Constraint among Pashtuns." *Journal of Peace Research* 34 (1): 53–71.

Johnson, Chalmers. 1964. *Revolution and the Social System*. Stanford, CA: Stanford University Press.

Johnston, Douglas. 1994. "Review of the Findings." In *Religion: The Missing Dimension of Statecraft*, edited by Douglas Johnston and Cynthia Sampson, 258–65. Oxford: Oxford University Press.London: Routledge.

Jongerden, Joost. 2001. "Resettlement and Reconstruction of Identity: The Case of the Kurds in Turkey." *Ethnopolitics* 1(1): 80–86.

Jongerden, Joost. 2007. *The Settlement Issue in Turkey and the Kurds: An Analysis of Spatial Politics, Modernity and War*. Leiden: Brill Academic.

Jongerden, Joost. 2016. "Colonialism, Self-Determination and Independence: The New PKK Paradigm." In *Kurdish Issues: Essays in Honor of Robert W. Olson*, edited by Michael M. Gunter, 106–21. Costa Mesa, CA: Mazda Publishers.

Jongerden, Joost. 2017. "The Kurdistan Workers Party (PKK): Radical Democracy and the Right to Self-Determination Beyond the Nation-State" In *The Kurdish Question Revisited*, edited by Gareth Stansfield and Mohammed Shareef. London: Hurst Publishers.

Jongerden, Joost, and Ahmet Hamdi Akkaya. 2011. "Born from the Left. The Making of the PKK." In *Nationalisms and Politics in Turkey: Political Islam, Kemalism and the Kurdish Issue*, edited by Marlies Casier and Joost Jongerden, 123–42.

Joshi, Madhav. 2010. "Post-Civil War Democratization: Promotion of Democracy in Post-Civil War States, 1946–2005." *Democratization* 17 (5): 826–55.

Juergensmeyer, Mark. 2017. *Terror in the Mind of God: The Global Rise of Religious Violence*. Oakland: University of California Press.

Jwaideh, Wadie. 2006. *The Kurdish National Movement: Its Origins and Development*. Syracuse, NY: Syracuse University Press.

Kafka, Franz. 1949. *The Diaries of Franz Kafka, 1914–1923*. New York: Schocken Books.

Kalyvas, N. Stathis. 2006. *The Logic of Violence in Civil War*. New York: Cambridge University Press.

Kandiyoti, Deniz. 1988. "Bargaining with Patriarchy." *Gender and Society* 2 (3): 274–90.

Kang, Seonjou, and James Meernik. 2005. "Civil War Destruction and the Prospects for Economic Growth." *Journal of Politics* 67 (1): 88–109.

Karam, Azza. 2001. "Women in War and Peace-building: The Roads Traversed, the Challenges Ahead." *International Feminist Journal of Politics* 3 (1): 2–25.

Kasapoglu, Cagil. 2015. "Agri'da AKP ile HDP'nin Nufuz Mucadelesi [AKP's Power Struggle with HDP in Agri.]" *BBC Turkce*, June 1, 2015, http://www.bbc.com/turkce/haberler/2015/06/150601_agri_secim_gs2015, accessed August 12, 2016.

Kaufman, Joyce P., and Kristen P. Williams. 2010. *Women and War: Gender Identity and Activism in Times of Conflict*. Sterling, VA: Kumarian Press.

Kaufmann, Chaim. 1996. "Possible and Impossible Solutions to Ethnic Civil Wars." *International Security* 20 (4): 136–75.

Kazemi, Farhad. 2000. "Gender, Islam, and Politics." *Social Research* 67 (2): 453–74.

Keen, David. 2005. *Conflict and Collusion in Sierra Leone*. New York: Palgrave.

Kibris, Arzu. 2011. "Funerals and Elections: The Effects of Terrorism on Voting Behavior in Turkey." *Journal of Conflict Resolution* 55 (2): 220–47.

Kibris, Arzu. 2015. "The Conflict Trap Revisited: Civil Conflict and Educational Achievement." *Journal of Conflict Resolution* 59 (4): 645–70.

Kibris, Arzu, and Nills Metternich. 2016. "The Flight of White-Collars: Civil Conflict, Availability of Medical Service Providers and Public Health." *Social Science and Medicine* 149: 93–103.

Kiras, James D. 2013. "Irregular Warfare: Terrorism and Insurgency." In *Strategy in the Contemporary World*, edited by John Baylis, James J. Wirtz, and Colin S. Gray, 174–92. Oxford: Oxford University Press.

Kisanak, Gultan, Nadje Al-Ali, and Latif Tas. 2016. "Kurdish Women's Battle Continues against State and Patriarchy, Says First Female Co-Mayor of Diyarbakir." *Open Democracy*, August 12, 2016, https://www.opendemocracy.net/nadje-al-ali-latif-tas-g-ltan-ki-anak/kurdish-women-s-battle-continues-against-state-and-patriarchy-, accessed August 26, 2016.

Knapp, Michael, Anja Flatch, and Ercan Ayboga. 2016. *Revolution in Rojava: Democratic Autonomy and Women's Liberation in the Syrian Kurdistan*. Chicago: University of Chicago Press.

Koc, Ismet, Attila Hancioglu, and Alanur Cavlin. 2008. "Demographic Differentials and Demographic Integration of Turkish and Kurdish Populations in Turkey." *Population Research and Policy Review* 27: 447–57.

KONDA 2010. Biz Kimiz'10 [Who Are We]. http://www.konda.com.tr/tr/raporlar.php?tb=3, accessed May 12, 2015.

Kose, Aynur, and Mustafa Yilmaz. 2012. "Flagging Turkishness: The Reproduction of Banal Nationalism in the Turkish Press." *Nationalities Papers* 40 (6): 909–25.

Kreutz, Joakim. 2010. "How Armed Conflicts End: Introducing the UCDP Conflict Termination Dataset." *Journal of Peace Research* 47 (2): 243–50.

Kundera, Milan. 1991. *Immortality*. New York: Grove Press.

Kurt, Mehmet. 2017. *Kurdish Hizbullah in Turkey: Islamism, Violence and the State*. Chicago: University of Chicago Press.

Lai, Brian, and Clayton Thyne. 2007. "The Effect of Civil War on Education, 1980–1997." *Journal of Peace Research* 44 (3): 277–92.

Laitin, D. David, and Rajesh Ramachandran. 2016. "Language Policy and Human Development." *American Political Science Review* 110 (3): 457–80.

Lasswell, Harold D. 1951. *The Political Writings of Harold D. Lasswell*. Glencoe, IL: Free Press.

Lemke, Douglas, and Jeff Carter. 2016. "Birth Legacies, State Making, and War." *Journal of Politics* 78 (2): 497–511.

Leverink, Joris. 2015. "Murray Bookchin and the Kurdish Resistance." *ROAR*, August 9, 2015, https://roarmag.org/essays/bookchin-kurdish-struggle-ocalan-rojava/, accessed August 5, 2016.

Licklider, Roy. 1995. "The Consequences of Negotiated Settlements in Civil Wars, 1945–1993." *American Political Science Review* 89 (3): 681–90.

Lowe, Robert. 2010. "The *Serhildan* and the Kurdish National Story in Syria." In *The Kurdish Policy Imperative*, edited by Robert Lowe and Gareth Stansfield, 161–79. London: Royal Institute of International Affairs.

Lyons, Terrence. 2016. "From Victorious Rebels to Strong Authoritarian Parties: Prospects for Post-War Democratization." *Democratization* 23 (6): 1026–41.

Makovsky, Alan. "Re-Educating Turkey: AKP Efforts to Promote Religious Values in Schools," https://cdn.americanprogress.org/wp-content/uploads/2015/12/09115835/Re-EducatingTurkey.pdf, accessed October 25, 2016.

Mampilly, Cherian Zachariah. 2011. *Rebel Rulers: Insurgent Governance and Civilian Life during War*. Ithaca, NY: Cornell University Press.

Mandiraci, Berkay. 2016. "Turkey's PKK Conflict: The Death Toll." *International Crisis Group*, July 20, 2016, http://blog.crisisgroup.org/europe-central-asia/2016/07/20/turkey-s-pkk-conflict-the-rising-toll/, accessed September 14, 2016.

Marcus, Aliza. 2007. *Blood and Belief: The PKK and Kurdish Fight for Independence*. New York: New York University Press.

Mason, T. David. 1992. "Women's Participation in Central American Revolutions: A Theoretical Perspective." *Comparative Political Studies* 25 (1): 63–89.

Mason, T. David, and Jerry A. Murtagh. 1985. "WHO RIOTS? An Empirical Examination of the 'New Urban Black' Versus the Social Marginality Hypotheses." *Political Behavior* 7 (4): 352–73.

McAdam, Dough, Sidney Tarrow, and Charles Tilly. 1996. "To Map Contentious Politics." *Mobilization: An International Journal* 1 (1): 17–34.

McCarthy, John D., and Mayer N. Zald. 1977. "Resource Mobilization and

Social Movements: A Partial Theory." *American Journal of Sociology* 82 (6): 1212–41.

McDowall, David. 2004. *A Modern History of the Kurds*. London: I. B. Tauris.

McKernan, Bethan. 2017. "Female Kurdish Fighters Announce New Training Academies for Arab Women to Take On Isis in Syria." *The Independent*, January 4, 2017, http://www.independent.co.uk/news/world/middle-east/female-kurdish-fighters-ypj-set-up-new-training-academies-arab-yazidi-women-to-fight-isis-a7508951.html, accessed January 5, 2017.

Menon, Nidhiya, and Yana van der Meulen Rodgers. 2015. "War and Women's Work: Evidence from the Conflict in Nepal." *Journal of Conflict Resolution* 59 (1): 51–73.

Moghadam, Valentine M. 2004. "The Gender of Democracy: The Link Between Women's Rights and Democratization in the Middle East." *Arab Reform Bulletin* 2 (7): 2–3.

Moore, Will H., and Stephen M. Shellman. 2004. "Fear of Persecution: Forced Migration, 1952–1995." *Journal of Conflict Resolution* 40 (5): 723–45.

Murdoch, J. C., and Todd Sandler. 2004. "Civil Wars and Economic Growth: Spatial Dispersion." *American Journal of Political Science* 48 (1): 138–51.

Mutlu, Servet. 1996. "Ethnic Kurds in Turkey: A Demographic Study." *International Journal of Middle East Studies* 28 (4): 517–41.

Neuberger, Benyamin. 2014. "Kurdish Nationalism in Comparative Perspective." In *Kurdish Awakening*, edited by Ofra Bengio, 15–35. Austin: University of Texas Press.

Newfield, Jack. 1966. *A Prophetic Minority*. New York: Signet.

Nietzsche, Friedrich. 2006. *On the Genealogy of Morality*. Translated by Carol Diethe. Edited by Keith Ansell-Pearson. Cambridge: Cambridge University Press.

Nilsson, Marcus. 2012. "Reaping What Was Sown: Conflict Outcome and Post–Civil War Democratization." *Cooperation and Conflict* 47 (3): 350–67.

Nordland, Rod. 2016. "Crackdown in Turkey Threatens a Haven of Gender Equality Built by Kurds." *The New York Times*, December 7, 2016, http://www.nytimes.com/2016/12/07/world/middleeast/turkey-kurds-womens-rights.html?ref=world&_r=0, accessed December 8, 2016.

Norris, Pippa, and Ronald Inglehart. 2004. *Sacred and Secular: Religion and Politics Worldwide*. Cambridge: Cambridge University Press.

Ocalan, Abdullah. 2011. *Democratic Confederalism*. London: Transmedia Publishing. Available at http://www.freeocalan.org/wp-content/uploads/2012/09/Ocalan-Democratic-Confederalism.pdf.

Ocalan, Abdullah. 2012. *War and Peace in Kurdistan*. Cologne, Germany: International Initiative. Available at http://www.freedom-for-ocalan.com/english/download/Ocalan-War-and-Peace-in-Kurdistan.pdf.

Ocalan, Abdullah. 2013. *Liberating Life: Women's Revolution*. Cologne, Germany: International Initiative. Available at http://www.freeocalan.org/wp-content/uploads/2014/06/liberating-Lifefinal.pdf.

Olson, Robert W. 1989a. *The Emergence of Kurdish Nationalism and the Sheikh Said Rebellion, 1880–1925*. Austin: University of Texas Press.

Olson, Robert W. 1989b. "The Kocgiri Kurdish Rebellion in 1921 and a Draft Law for a Proposed Autonomy of Kurdistan." *Oriente Moderno* 8 (69): 41–56.

Olson, Robert W. 2001. *Turkey's Relations with Iran, Syria, Israel and Russia, 1991–2000*. Costa Mesa, CA: Mazda Publishers.

Oran, Baskin. 2006. *Kenan Evren'in Yazilmamis Anilari* [Kenan Evren's Unpublished Diaries]. Istanbul: Iletisim.

Ozturk, Ahmet Erdi. 2016. "'Turkey' Diyanet under AKP rule: from protector to imposer of state ideology?" *Southeast European and Black Sea Studies* 16 (4): 619–635.

Palmieri, Patrick A., Katie J. Chipman, Daphna Canetti, Robert J. Johnson, and Stevan E. Hobfall. 2010. *Journal of Clinical Sleep Medicine* 6 (6): 557–64.

Pankhurst, Donna. 2003. "The 'Sex War' and Other Wars: Toward a Feminist Approach to Peacebuilding," *Development in Practice* 13 (2–3): 154–77.

Pearlman, Wendy. 2016. "Narratives of Fear in Syria." *Perspectives on Politics* 14 (1): 21–37.

Pham, Phuong N., Harvey M. Weinstein, and Timothy Longman. 2004. "Trauma and PTSD Symptoms in Rwanda: Implications for Attitudes Toward Justice and Reconciliation." *Journal of American Medical Association (JAMA)* 292 (5): 602–12.

Philipose, Liz. 2007. "The Politics of Pain and the End of Empire." *International Feminist Journal of Politics* 9 (1): 60–81.

Phillips, David. 2017. "Turkey's Referendum: Free and Fair?" *Huffington Post*, April 14, 2017, http://www.huffingtonpost.com/entry/58f0eba3e4b0156697224ea7, accessed April 14, 2017.

Philpott, Daniel. 2007. "Explaining the Political Ambivalence of Religion." *American Political Science Review* 101 (3): 505–525.

Posner, N. Daniel. 2004. "The Political Salience of Cultural Difference: Why Chewas and Tumbukas Are Allies in Zambia and Adversaries in Malawi." *American Political Science Review* 98 (4): 529–45.

Quinn, Michael J., T. David Mason, Mehmet Gurses. 2007. "Sustaining the Peace: Determinants of Civil War Recurrence." *International Interactions* 33 (2): 167–93.

Rafter, Nicole. 2016. *The Crime of All Crimes: Toward a Criminology of Genocide*. New York: New York University Press.

Ramazani, Nesta. 1993. "Women in Iran: The Revolutionary Ebb and Flow." *Middle East Journal* 47 (3): 409–28.

Rezai-Rashti, Goli M. 2015. "The Politics of Gender Segregation and Women's Access to Higher Education in the Islamic Republic of Iran: The Inter-play of Repression and Resistance." *Gender and Education* 27 (5): 469–86.

Richards, Paul. 1995. "Rebellion in Liberia and Sierra Leone: A Crisis of Youth?" In *Conflict in Africa*, edited by Oliver Furley, 134–70. London: I. B. Tauris.

Robins-Early, Nick. 2015. "Meet the HDP, the Pro-Gay, Pro-Women Kurdish Party Shaking up Turkish Politics." *Huffington Post*, June 11, 2015, http://www.huffingtonpost.com/2015/06/08/turkey-hdp-party_n_7537648.html, accessed September 26, 2016.

Rohner, Dominic, Mathias Thoenig, and Fabrizio Zilibotti. 2013. "Seeds of Distrust: Conflict in Uganda." *Journal of Economic Growth* 18: 217–52.

Romano, David. 2006. *The Kurdish Nationalist Movement: Opportunity, Mobilization and Identity*. Cambridge: Cambridge University Press.

Romano, David, and Mehmet Gurses. 2014. *Conflict, Democratization, and the Kurds in the Middle East: Turkey, Iran, Iraq, and Syria*. New York: Palgrave Macmillan.

Ross, Michael. 2006. "A Closer Look at Oil, Diamonds, and Civil War." *Annual Review of Political Science* 9 (June): 265–300.

Rueveny, Rafael, Andreea S. Mihalache-O'Keef, and Quan Li. 2010. "The Effects of Warfare on the Environment." *Journal of Peace Research* 47 (6): 749–61.

Rumelili, Bahar, and Ayse Betul Celik. 2017. "Ontological Insecurity in Asymmetric Conflicts: Reflections on Agonistic Peace in Turkey's Kurdish Issue." *Security Dialogue* 1–18. DOI: 10.1177/0967010617695715.

Rustow, Dankwart A. 1970. "Transitions to Democracy: Toward a Dynamic Model." *Comparative Politics* 2 (3): 337–63.

Sabanci, A. Ahmet. 2015. "Walls of Silvan: The Dark Story of the 12-Day Curfew." *Voice of Jiyan*, November 15, 2015, http://voiceofjiyan.com/2015/11/15/walls-of-silvan-tell-the-dark-story-of-the-12-day-curfew/, accessed December 12, 2016.

Sack, William H., Gregory N. Clarke, and John Seeley. 1996. "Multiple Forms of Stress in Cambodian Adolescent Refugees." *Child Development* 67 (1): 107–16.

Sahin-Mencutek, Zeynep. 2016. "Strong in the Movement, Strong in the Party: Women's Representation in the Kurdish Party of Turkey." *Political Studies* 64 (2): 470–87.

Saideman, M. Stephen, and R. William Ayres. 2000. "Determining the Causes of Irredentism: Logit Analyses of Minorities at Risk Data from the 1980s and 1990s." *Journal of Politics* 62 (4): 1126–44.

Salehyan, Idean. 2007. "Transnational Rebels: Neighboring States as Sanctuary for Rebel Groups." *World Politics* 59 (1): 217–42.

Sambanis, Nicholas. 2000. "Partition as a Solution to Ethnic War: An Empirical Critique of the Theoretical Literature." *World Politics* 52 (4): 437–83.

Sambanis, Nicholas. 2001. "Do Ethnic and Nonethnic Civil Wars Have the Same Causes? A Theoretical and Empirical Inquiry (Part 1)." *Journal of Conflict Resolution* 45 (3): 259–82.

Sambanis, Nicholas. 2004. "What Is Civil War? Conceptual and Empirical Complexities of an Operational Definition." *Journal of Conflict Resolution* 18 (6): 814–58.

Sambanis, Nicholas, and Jonah Schulhofer-Wohl. 2009. "What's in a Line? Is Partition a Solution to Civil War?" *International Security* 34 (2): 82–118.

Sampson, Cynthia. 1994. "'To Make Real the Bond Between Us All': Quaker Conciliation During the Nigerian Civil War." In *Religion: The Missing Dimension of Statecraft*, edited by Douglas Johnston and Cynthia Sampson, 88–118. Oxford: Oxford University Press.

Sandal, Nukhet Ahu. 2011. "Religious Actors as Epistemic Communities in Conflict Transformation: The Cases of South Africa and Northern Ireland." *Review of International Studies* 37: 929–49.

Saracoglu, Cenk. 2009. "'Exclusive Recognition': The New Dimensions of the Question of Ethnicity and Nationalism in Turkey." *Ethnic and Racial Studies* 32 (4): 640–58.

Sarigil, Zeki, and Omer Fazlioglu. 2013. "Religion and Ethno-nationalism: Turkey's Kurdish Issue." *Nations and Nationalism* 19 (3): 551–71.

Sarigil, Zeki, and Ekrem Karakoc. 2016. "Who Supports Secession: The Determinants of Secessionist Attitudes among Turkey's Kurds." *Nations and Nationalism* 22 (2): 325–46.

Sarkees, Meredith Reid, and Frank Wayman. 2010. *Resort to War: 1816–2007*. Washington, DC: CQ Press.

Scholte, Willem F., Miranda Olff, Peter Ventevogel, Giel-Jan de Vries, Eveline Jansveld, Barbara Lopes Cardozo, and Carol A. Gotway Crawford. 2004. "Mental Health Symptoms Following War and Repression in Eastern Afghanistan." *Journal of American Medical Association (JAMA)* 292 (5): 585–93.

Sharma, Suraj. 2016. "Kurdish Club becomes Political as it Chases Turkish Cup Dream." *Middle East Eye*, February 8, 2016, http://www.middleeasteye.net/Turkey%20football%20politics%20Amedspor, accessed December 12, 2016.

Sheehan, Neil. 1988. *A Bright Shining Lie: John Paul Vann and America in Vietnam*. New York: Random House.

Smelser, Neil J. 1963. *Theory of Collective Behavior*. New York: Free Press.

Solati, Fariba. 2017. *Women, Work, and Patriarchy in the Middle East and North Africa*. Cham, Switzerland: Palgrave Macmillan.

Soleimani, Kamal. 2016. *Islam and Competing Nationalism in the Middle East, 1876–1926*. New York: Palgrave Macmillan.

Somasundaram, Daya. 1998. *Scarred Minds: The Psychological Impacts of War on Sri Lankan Tamils*. New Delhi: Sage Publications.

Somer, Murat. 2005. "Failures of the Discourse of Ethnicity: Turkey, Kurds, and the Emerging Iraq." *Security Dialogue* 36 (1): 109–28.

Somer, Murat. 2010. "Media Values and Democratization: What Unites and What Divides Religious-Conservative and Pro-Secular Elites?" *Turkish Studies* 11 (4): 555–77.

Somer, Murat. 2016. "Conquering Versus Democratizing the State: Political Islamists and Fourth Wave Democratization in Turkey and Tunisia." *Democratization* http://dx.doi.org/10.1080/13510347.2016.1259216.

Somer, Murat, and Evangelos G. Liaras. 2010. "Turkey's New Kurdish Opening: Religious Versus Secular Values." *Middle East Policy* XVII (2): 152–65.

Stewart, Megan A. 2015. "Civil War as State-Building: The Determinants of Insurgent Public Goods Provision." Paper presented at International Studies Association Annual Meeting, February 18–21, 2015. http://web.isanet.org/Web/Conferences/New%20Orleans%202015/Archive/d2a4ea56-309f-42b4-b2d1-74772af1f9b2.pdf, accessed August 21, 2016.

Svensson, Isak. 2007. "Fighting with Faith: Religion and Conflict Resolution in Civil Wars." *Journal of Conflict Resolution* 15 (6): 930–49.

Talhami, Ghada Hashem. 1996. *The Mobilization of Muslim Women in Egypt.* Gainesville: University of Florida Press.

Tansey, Oisin. 2007. "Process Tracing and Elite Interviewing: A Case for Non-Probability Sampling." *PS: Political Science and Politics* 40 (4): 765–72.

Tax, Meredith. 2016a. *A Road Unforeseen: Women Fight the Islamic State.* New York: Bellevue Literary Press.

Tax, Meredith. 2016b. "Turkey Is Supporting the Syrian Jihadis Washington Says It Wants to Fight." *The Nation*, September 16, 2016, https://www.the-nation.com/article/turkey-is-supporting-the-syrian-jihadis-washington-says-it-wants-to-fight/, accessed September 16, 2016.

Taylor, Charles. 2011. "Western Secularity." In *Rethinking Secularism*, edited by Craig Calhoun, Mark Juergensmeyer, and Jonathan VanAntwerpen, 31–53. Oxford: Oxford University Press.

Tedeschi, Richard G., and Lawrence G. Calhoun. 1996. "The Posttraumatic Growth Inventory." *Journal of Traumatic Stress* 9 (3): 455–71.

Tedeschi, Richard G., and Lawrence G. Calhoun. 2004. "Posttraumatic Growth: Conceptual Foundations and Empirical Evidence." *Psychological Inquiry* 15 (1): 1–18.

Tejel, Jordi. 2016. "Beyond the Dichotomy of Accommodation Versus Resistance: The Kurdish Minority in Iraq and Syria in Long-Term and Comparative Perspectives, 1920–2015." In *Kurdish Issues: Essays in Honor of Robert W. Olson*, edited by Michael M. Gunter, 258–82. Costa Mesa, CA: Mazda Publishers.

Tezcur, Gunes Murat. 2014. "The Ebb and Flow of Armed Conflict in Turkey: An Elusive Peace." In *Conflict, Democratization, and the Kurds in the Middle*

East: Turkey, Iran, Iraq, and Syria, edited by David Romano and Mehmet Gurses, 171–88. New York: Palgrave Macmillan.

Tezcur, Gunes Murat, and Mehmet Gurses. 2017. "Ethnic Exclusion and Mobilization: The Kurdish Conflict in Turkey." *Comparative Politics* 49 (2): 213–30.

Thames, Frank C., and Margaret S. Williams. 2015. *Contagious Representation Women's Political Representation in Democracies around the World.* New York: New York University Press.

Tilly, Charles. 1975. "Reflections on the History of European State-Making." In *The Formation of National States in Western Europe*, edited by Charles Tilly, 3–83. Princeton, NJ: Princeton University Press.

Tilly, Charles. 1978. *From Mobilization to Revolution.* Reading, MA: Addison-Wesley.

Tilly, Charles. 1990. *Coercion, Capital, and European States, AD 990–1990.* Cambridge, MA: Basil Blackwell.

Tilly, Charles. 1998. "Where Do Rights Come From?" In *Democracy, Revolution and History*, edited by Theda Skocpol, 55–72. Ithaca, NY: Cornell University Press.

Tilly, Charles. 2002. *Stories, Identities, and Political Change.* Lanham, MD: Rowman and Littlefield.

Tilly, Charles. 2008. *Contentious Performances.* Cambridge: Cambridge University Press.

Tilly, Charles. 2012. *Stories, Identities, and Political Change.* Lanham, MD: Rowman & Littlefield.

Toft, Monica Duffy. 2007. "Getting Religion? The Puzzling Case of Islam and Civil War." *International Security* 31 (4): 97–131.

Toft, Monica Duffy, Daniel Philpott, Timothy Samuel Shah. 2011. *God's Century: Resurgent Religion and Global Politics.* New York, NY: Norton & Company.

Toivanen, Mari, and Bahar Baser. 2016. "Gender in the Representations of an Armed Conflict: Female Kurdish Combatants in French and British Media." *Middle East Journal of Culture and Communication* 9: 294–314.

Tønder, Lars. 2013. *Tolerance: A Sensorial Orientation to Politics.* Oxford: Oxford University Press.

Tripp, Aili Mari. 2000. *Women & Politics in Uganda.* Madison: University of Wisconsin Press.

Tripp, Aili Mari. 2015. *Women and Power in Postconflict Africa.* Cambridge: Cambridge University Press.

Ulug, Melis Ozden, and J. Christopher Cohrs. 2017. "Examining the Ethos of Conflict by Exploring Lay People's Representations of the Kurdish Conflict in Turkey." *Conflict Management and Peace Science* DOI: 10.1177/0738894216674969.

Uvuza, Justine N. 2014. "Hidden Inequalities: Rwandan Female Politicians' Experiences of Balancing Family and Political Responsibilities." PhD Dissertation, Newcastle University, https://theses.ncl.ac.uk/dspace/bitstream/10443/2475/1/Uvuza,%20J.%2014.pdf, accessed August 12, 2016.

Vali, Abbas. 2016. "Reflections on Kurdish Society and Politics in Rojhelat: An Overview." In *Kurdish Issues: Essays in Honor of Robert W. Olson*, edited by Michael M. Gunter, 283–314. Costa Mesa, CA: Mazda Publishers.

Viterna, Jocelyn. 2014. *Women in War: The Micro Processes of Mobilization in El Salvador*. New York: Oxford University Press.

Volkan, Vamik D. 1979. "Symptom Formation and Character Changes Due to Upheavals of War: Examples from Cyprus." *American Journal of Psychotherapy* 33 (2): 239–62.

Volkan, Vamik. 1996. *Bloodlines: From Ethnic Pride to Ethnic Terrorism*. Boulder, CO: Westview Press.

Voors, Maarten J., Eleonora E. M. Nillesen, Philip Verwimp, Erwin H. Bulte, Robert Lensink, and Daan P. Van Soest. 2012. "Violent Conflict and Behavior: A Field Experiment in Burundi." *American Economic Review* 102 (2): 941–64.

Wallensteen, Peter. 2015. *Quality Peace: Peacebuilding, Victory, and World Order*. New York: Oxford University Press.

Wantchekon, Leonard. 2004. "The Paradox of 'Warlord' Democracy: A Theoretical Investigation." *American Political Science Review* 9 (1): 17–33.

Weber, Max. 1946. "Politics as a Vocation." In *From Max Weber: Essays in Sociology*, edited by H. H. Gerth and C. Wright Mills, 77–128. New York: Oxford University Press.

Weidman, B. Nils. 2009. "Geography as Motivation and Opportunity: Group Concentration and Ethnic Conflict." *Journal of Peace Research* 53 (4): 526–43.

Westrheim, Kariane. 2014. "Taking to the Street!: Kurdish Collective Action in Turkey." In *The Kurdish Question in Turkey: New Perspectives on Violence, Representation, and Reconciliation*, edited by Cengiz Gunes and Welat Zeydanlioglu, 136–61. London: Routledge.

White, Paul. 2015. *The PKK: Coming Down from the Mountains*. London: Zed Books.

Wimmer, Andreas. 2013. *Waves of War: Nationalism, State Formation, and Ethnic Exclusion in the Modern World*. New York: Cambridge University Press.

Wimmer, Andreas, Lars-Erik Cederman, and Brian Min. 2009. "Ethnic Politics and Armed Conflict: A Global Configurational Analysis of a New Global Data Set." *American Sociological Review* 74 (2): 316–37.

Wirth, Louis. 1936. "Preface." In *Ideology and Utopia: An Introduction to the Sociology of Knowledge*, edited by Karl Mannheim. London: Harcourt, Brace and Company.

Wood, Elisabeth J. 2000. *Forging Democracy From Below: Insurgent Transitions in South Africa and El Salvador*. New York: Cambridge University Press.

Wood, Elisabeth J. 2001. "An Insurgent Path To Democracy: Popular Mobilization, Economic Interests, and Regime Transition in South Africa and El Salvador." *Comparative Political Studies* 34 (8): 862–88.

Wood, Elisabeth J. 2003. *Insurgent Collective Action and Civil War in El Salvador*. New York: Cambridge University Press.

Wood, Elisabeth J. 2008. "The Social Process of Civil War: The Wartime Transformation of Social Networks." *Annual Review of Political Science* 11: 539–61.

Wood, M. Reed, and Jakana L. Thomas. 2017. "Women on the Frontline: Rebel Group Ideology and Women's Participation in Violent Rebellion." *Journal of Peace Research* 54 (1): 31–46.

Yackley, Jean Ayla. 2015. "Gay, Christian, Roma Election Candidates Show Turkey's Changing Face." *Reuters*, June 5, 2015, http://www.reuters.com/article/us-turkey-election-minorities-idUSKBN0OL1BN20150605, accessed December 18, 2016.

Yamane, Taro. 1967. *Statistics: An Introductory Analysis*, 2nd ed., New York: Harper and Row.

Yanarocak, Hay Eytan Cohen. 2014. "A Tale of Political Consciousness: The Rise of a Nonviolent Kurdish Political Movement in Turkey." In *Kurdish Awakening*, edited by Ofra Bengio, 137–54. Austin: University of Texas Press.

Yanarocak, Hay Eytan Cohen. 2016. "The Indoctrination and Socialization of Ataturkism in Turkish Education System and the School Textbooks, 1980–2012." Dissertation Thesis. Tel-Aviv University.

Yegen, Mesut. 1996. "The Turkish State Discourse and the Exclusion of Kurdish Identity." *Middle Eastern Studies* 32 (2): 216–29.

Yegen, Mesut. 2007. "Turkish Nationalism and the Kurdish Question." *Ethnic and Racial Studies* 30 (1): 119–51.

Yetkin, Murat. 2008. "Genelkurmay Baskani Basbug: Asker Uzerinden Siyaset Yapmayin" [Chief of Staff Basbug: Don't Drag the Military into Politics], *Radikal*, September 17, 2008, http://www.radikal.com.tr/yazarlar/murat-yetkin/genelkurmay-baskani-basbug-asker-uzerinden-siyaset-yapma-yin-899070/, accessed January 30, 2017.

Yuksel, Sahika, and Tuba Olgun-Ozpolat. 2004. "Psychological Problems Associated with Traumatic Loss in Turkey." *Bereavement Care* 23 (1): 5–7, DOI: 10.1080/02682620408657592.

Zeb, Rizwan. 2006. "Pakistan and Jihadi Groups in the Kashmir Conflict." In *Kashmir: New Voices, New Approaches*, edited by Waheguru Pal Singh Sidhu, Bushra Asif, and Cyrus Samii, 65–77. Boulder, CO: Lynne Rienner.

Index